# The Faery
# British Music

## John Kruse

# Contents

## Intro: Faes on Stage

Faeries have profoundly shaped the arts for centuries. They have been the subject of paintings, poems and plays- from *Midsummer Night's Dream* to *Peter Pan*.

Faeries are part of the British cultural experience and, as such, they are a powerful element in all the expressions of that culture. Britishness, in literature or in music, is intimately bound up with King Arthur, Avalon, folk culture and folk tradition. Few people may be morris dancers- or enjoy the custom- but it symbolises something unique to the British Isles. If you want to conjure deeply affecting images of Britishness, allusions to the mysteries of Faery and to the magic of Avalon are highly effective ways of doing so. Connections are triggered, chords are struck, and two thousand years of culture are brought to bear- concisely and powerfully.

Even in the twenty first century, Faery continues to affect our art and culture. There is a continuing thirst for dramatic representations of Tolkien's Middle Earth and the wider appetite for fantasy literature feeds a similar interest in elves and faeries in contemporary music. It would be quite wrong to suppose that grime, rap and other such genres have diminished the taste for the supernatural in rock and pop. It persists, vigorous and continually creative.

This book is dedicated to the memory of my mother, who took me as a child to see amateur productions of Gilbert and Sullivan and *The Magic Flute;* later, when I was a young teenager, she bought my first proper album for me, Mike Oldfield's *Tubular Bells.* She thought this purchase marked the failure of her attempts to educate me about 'good music,' but her influence underlies much of this book.

# Classical Music

Faery plays, and musical interpretations of faery texts, have always been closely related. Composer Henry Purcell based his 1692 masque *The Fairy Queen* very loosely on Shakespeare's *Midsummer Night's Dream*. The Pyramus and Thisbe scenes were excised from the same text by Richard Leveridge so as to create a burlesque opera that was staged in 1716 and 1745. Another operatic version of the play appeared in 1816. It was only in 1840 that audiences once again got to see nearly the whole of Shakespeare's drama as it had originally been written, when the actress Lucia Vestris produced the play at Covent Garden- but, even then, the performance added musical sequences and ballet to the straightforward drama.

Faery king Oberon, familiar to us from *Midsummer Night's Dream,* had in fact been borrowed by Shakespeare from a French medieval romance, *Huon of Bordeaux.* This story was given new life in Germany in 1780 by the publication of Christoph Martin Wieland's epic poem *Oberon,* which marked the beginning of a reinvigorated interest in the story. Actress Friedericke Sophie Seyler used the verses from Wieland's work to create a *Singspiel* titled *Huon und Amande,* which in turn was copied in 1789 to form the libretto for the opera, *Oberon, König der Elfen*, by the Austrian composer Paul Wranitzky. Another German composer, Carl Maria von Weber, also used the poem as the basis for an opera, *Oberon- or the Elf King's Oath*, in 1826. Other operatic versions of the romance include William Sotheby's *Oberon, or a Mask in Five Parts* (1803), the anonymous *The Gnome King: An Elfin Freak, or Legend of Number-Nip* (1819) and George Macfarren's *Oberon, or the Charmed Horn* (1826). Wieland's work was also adapted into a ballet, *Sire Huon,* by Michael Costa in 1834. Inspiration travelled in the opposite direction as well. Felix Mendelssohn composed music for a version of *The Dream* based upon a translation into German by August Wilhelm Schlegel and Ludwig Tieck. Germanic legend was used as the basis of opera by Jacques Offenbach (*The Rhein Fairies,* 1864), whilst Richard Wagner wrote *Die Feen* (The Fairies) in 1833 and *Tannhäuser* in 1845.

As will be seen, faery, in some form or other, had long been regarded as a proper subject for serious musical composition.

## Gilbert and Sullivan

There might be a case for dealing with Gilbert and Sullivan's Savoy operas under popular music, given their lyrics, but Sir Arthur Sullivan's' musical scores place them more squarely in the classical tradition.

*Iolanthe, or, The Peer and the Peri,* was the seventh comic opera written for the Savoy theatre by composer Sullivan and librettist W. S. Gilbert. It was first performed in November 1882, when the production employed the latest technology to give the fairies sparkling wands and wreaths on their heads lit with electricity.

The new opera was a huge success, but it was very far from being the first time that Walter Gilbert had made use of fairy themes. Very many of his works involve magic, whilst he had first demonstrated an interest in faerylore in one of his *Bab Ballads,* a song called the *Fairy Curate,* which was published in July 1870. This concerned a "fairy/ Light and airy" who marries a mortal and has a son. He, in time, becomes a clergyman, even though he has wings and can fly to visit his mother. Ultimately, he is dismissed from his living (and becomes a Mormon) because his bishop refuses to believe that he is not involved with a twenty-year-old ballet dancer when he himself is already a good deal older (this female was, of course, his ageless mother).

At Christmas 1874, Gilbert published a short story, 'The Story of a Twelfth Cake,' in *The Graphic*, a weekly illustrated newspaper. The piece concerned a man who, with the help of a fairy, changes a small event in his past in order to try to save his engagement. However, this revision causes profound alterations in the present, which only make his situation even worse. Gilbert recycled this plot seven years later, for in mid-December 1881 *Foggerty's Fairy- An Entirely Original Fairy Farce*, opened at the Criterion Theatre in Piccadilly, London. Despite some favourable reviews, the production closed after barely two dozen performances. Discouraged, Gilbert turned back to writing comic operas with Arthur Sullivan, staging *Iolanthe* less than a year later.

At the core of *Foggerty's Fairy* is fairy magic. Foggerty wishes he had a guardian angel to rescue him from his predicament, and discovers that, in fact, he has a good fairy guardian, called Rebecca. At first, however, he can't believe that she's real- even though she just has appeared by entering the room through a solid wall, carrying a wand. She complains:

> "it's the old story. Nobody believes in us nowadays. Time was when we mixed ourselves up, as a matter of course, in human business. We were a power then, and people were afraid of us. Whenever an important christening took place, we were invited as a matter of course, and if any one of us was neglected, it was bad for the baby. Ah, those were days!"

Foggerty still refuses to accept Rebecca's reality, so she explains simply that she is his "tutelary fairy - your guardian genius. I hover over you [literally- and at all times]." She wants to help him- but within limits. He has been involved with an older woman, whom he now wants out of the way so he can marry someone much younger. Rebecca acknowledges that a bad fairy would happily strangle the old flame- something that she as a good fairy simply cannot contemplate. She can however, edit his past so that he never meets the woman- although Rebecca warns that this will "blot out at the same time all the consequences that came of having known her." Rebecca provides him with some magical pills and a potion and, with another warning about the consequences of changing his past, departs: "Well, I must be off now, for I've got to dance second in a ballet in a fairy glen in half an hour." Foggerty uses the magical pills to undo his past, but the effect of that, necessarily, is also to release Rebecca from any responsibility for him as his guardian.

Despite the failure of *Foggerty's Fairy,* Gilbert was plainly reluctant to relinquish faes and their magic as a plot device within his world of topsy-turvy. The plot of *Iolanthe,* written shortly afterwards, concerns the fairy Iolanthe, who has been banished from fairyland for the last twenty-five years because she had married a mortal, an act forbidden by fairy law. Her son, Strephon, is an Arcadian shepherd who wants to marry Phyllis, a ward of the court of Chancery. All the members of the House of Peers also want to marry her. Then, unfortunately, Phyllis sees Strephon hugging a young woman and- not realising that it is his mother, who as an immortal being always retains her youth- she assumes the worst: that he, a twenty-five-year-old, has fallen for a girl of seventeen. This sets off a climactic confrontation between the peers and the fairies, which forms a satire of British government and society. It also permits a mild pun upon 'peer' and the Persian term for a supernatural being 'peri.'

Building upon his earlier faery works, Gilbert's the libretto deploys to the full all the conventions of Victorian faery-lore. At the very start of the first act, the chorus appear, declaring that "We must dance and we must sing/ Round about our fairy ring!" It is, in fact, Iolanthe who has composed these songs and measures for her sister faes. Gilbert's fairies are, we learn, winged and are endowed with the power of changing their size- for example, to be able to creep through keyholes. Two solos follow the first appearance of the chorus, sung by the fairies Celia and Leila:

"We are dainty little fairies,
Ever singing, ever dancing;
We indulge in our vagaries
In a fashion most entrancing.

9

If you ask the special function
Of our never-ceasing motion,
We reply, without compunction,
That we haven't any notion!"

"If you ask us how we live,
Lovers all essentials give-
We can ride on lovers' sighs,
Warm ourselves in lovers' eyes,
Bathe ourselves in lovers' tears,
Clothe ourselves with lovers' fears,
Arm ourselves with lovers' darts,
Hide ourselves in lovers' hearts.
When you know us, you'll discover
That we almost live on lover!"

The flippancy of these lines is very typical of Gilbert; the intimate connection that's made with human affairs of the heart is not entirely his- there are hints of it in Tudor and Stuart materials- but he exaggerates it, very much in line with the Victorian trend of making faeries feminine, delicate and romantically charming, but largely harmless. That said, the Fairy Queen at one point threatens to "launch from fairy portals/ All the most terrific thunders/ In my armoury of wonders!" This control over the weather is very likely to have been borrowed from Titania in *Midsummer Night's Dream*.[1]

Over twenty years after *Iolanthe*, Gilbert yet again reverted to a fairy theme, with *Harlequin and the Fairy's Dilemma*, a two act play that was retitled as *The Fairy's Dilemma* shortly after it opened. It was staged at the Garrick Theatre in Charing Cross Road, London, was well received, and then ran for ninety performances between May and July 1904.

Once again, the origin for this "original domestic pantomime in two acts" was a short story Gilbert had published in *The Graphic* for Christmas 1900. Central to the play is the good

[1] Michael Ffinch, *Gilbert & Sullivan,* 1993, 102-119.

fairy Rosebud, who is depressed because the Fairy Queen has told her that her incompetence will no longer be tolerated. Unless she becomes more attentive to her duties- which are guiding the course true love between human couples, and protecting them from the interference of demons- she "shall be relegated to dance in the back rows with the stout ones." Rosebud, with her wings and her moral responsibilities, is evidently rather more like an angel (or even a Cupid) than any sort of faery we might recognise from British tradition.

The play jokingly distinguishes between the supernaturals (demons, fairies, goblins and imps) and the un-naturals (the humans). The faeries are female (and plainly willowy), they are dressed in short tutus like ballet dancers, and they always speak in rhyme. They can appear and disappear at will and they wield their magical powers through their wands, so as to resolve problems in human affairs of the heart.

Perhaps due to the success of *The Fairy's Dilemma*, Gilbert was still not done with Faery. Within just a few years, he had written a two-act comic opera, *Fallen Fairies, or, The Wicked World*. His partnership with Sullivan had ended and the score was supplied by Edward German. The libretto is an adaptation of Gilbert's 1873 blank-verse comedy, *The Wicked World*. The fairies- who are (again) very like angels in their moral conduct- are shocked but fascinated by the sinful behaviour of mortals, particularly their strange capacity for love (an emotion with which the faes are unfamiliar). They summon three mortal men both to observe them and to teach them how to live virtuously. The fairies fall in love with these mortals, but become jealous of each other and start to behave badly. The story concludes when the men return to Earth, leaving the fairies to realise that love is overrated. The opera opened at the Savoy in December 1909, but was not a success. It effectively spelled an end to Gilbert's career in opera (although he died two years later in any case).

The fairyland of this final opera is situated above the clouds, out of contact with our corrupted world (as was also the case

11

in *Foggerty's Fairy*).  It is an almost entirely female realm except for a servant called Lutin, a name taken from French folklore, and denoting a type of hobgoblin.  The faery queen is named Selene, after the Greek moon goddess, and her subjects are winged and can fly.  There is, therefore, little original or novel about the faes except for their complete lack of familiarity with love (in stark contrast to the fairies of *Iolanthe*).  This aspect of their character connects them to traditional British faes, but in this case it derives from their angelic purity, rather than the amoral and selfish nature of the fairy of folklore.

Musical Theatre

The comic operas of Gilbert and Sullivan had some 'artistic' aspirations.  Other productions, combining drama and song, were intended purely as entertainment and were aimed largely at children.

At Christmas 1901, J. M. Barrie was amongst the audience at the Vaudeville Theatre, on The Strand in London, to see a new production, *Bluebell in Fairyland,* an event which directly inspired his own play *Peter Pan*.[2]  *Bluebell in Fairyland* was one of the first stage plays written specifically for a child audience.  Its plot is insubstantial, though: Bluebell is a poor flower seller who cares for her two younger sisters.  One evening at Christmas she starts to read them a fairy tale but falls asleep part of the way through.  In her dream she visits fairyland, has some adventures, and then awakens.  The story ends happily with Bluebell and her sisters being adopted by a rich old man and with her marriage to Dicky the bootblack.

A number of incidents in the play are of general interest.  The Good Fairy sends a wicked king into a long sleep because he is a miser and has neglected the poor of his realm, whilst Bluebell is rewarded because she has been good; this may draw upon the British tradition that fairies prefer the generous

---

[2] *Bluebell in Fairyland,* Seymour Hicks, 1901.

and kind.  There is a cat, called Peter, who is a fairy and can speak.  This may just be fancy, to appeal to children, but it may, too, draw on the folk tale of the 'King of the Cats.'  Disrespect to the fairies meets with slaps from invisible hands, a very typical fairy response.

There is, too, plenty of mere whimsy designed to make the junior audience laugh.  The denizens of fairy land are "the very best kind of fairies.  They only have one evening out a week and do their own washing."  The sleeping king is guarded by a yellow dwarf whose 'general business manager' is a talking owl.  The fairies' stage costumes reflect contemporary conceptions- ones which still apply days: the Will of the Wisp is dressed in "a pretty fairylike dancing dress" and the Good Fairy wears "silver spangles and muslin, with a star on her head and a wand."  All the fairies were played by young females.

The fairies in *Bluebell in Fairyland* are associated with music, which was represented by the tinkling of bells, and a number of songs intersperse the dialogue.  Fairyland and dreamland are directly equated: children travel there when they sleep, so that in one song we hear that:

> "Eye-lids droop and close as darkness falls
> Fairyland is waiting when the dustman calls."

Faery is a place that can only be visited at night- an authentic detail.  It is the sprinkling of magic golden dust that sends the children to sleep and permits them to drift away on journey to a place where:

> "There's a land of golden weather
> At the dreaming journey's end;
> For the sun is always shining
> And the skies are always blue
> When each cloud has a silver lining
> And the fairy tales come true."[3]

Very evidently, the Faery that Bluebell visits is some sort of paradise, where all is kindness and love (unlike the fairyland of British folklore, which is a far less friendly place). We'll encounter the notion of dust transporting children to Faery again a little later, when we come to consider Edward Elgar's adaptation of Algernon Blackwood's 1913 novel, *A Prisoner in Fairyland,* another work which must surely owe a debt to *Bluebell.*

Music as a traditional adjunct of faery is seen again later in the play when Bluebell awakens the fairy king from his three-hundred-year slumber, singing:

> "Peal, golden bells
> Let your music ring
> From fairyland spells
> To waken a king."

The little flower-seller's voice is sufficient to break the spell that has bound the king for centuries.[4]

Bluebell's fairyland is a comforting and benign place, an escape from some of the harsh realities of an unequal and unfair world. Within a decade and a half, though, it was no longer possible to shield even the most well-off children from some of the cruelties of life. In Spring 1917 the Germans began to use Gotha heavy bombers to carry out air raids against the South-East of England. In response, Rose Patry wrote the play *Britain's Defenders, or Peggy's Peep into Fairyland, a Fairy Play,* which was published with a musical score in autumn that year.

The play concerns Peggy and her sister Betty, who sneak out of their beds and into a nearby dell in the hope of seeing the fairies dancing in a fairy ring. Instead, they see various fairies

---

[3] Act II, scene 1.
[4] Act II, scene 3.

of the natural world, along with Britannia, lead in the Moon as a prisoner. The Moon's offence has been to shine at night and to show the German bombers the way to their targets. The assembled fairies sing:

"Oh, naughty Moon, you are in disgrace,
Mind you be good and hide your face;
When Gothas o'er the North Sea fly,
Go bye-bye, go bye-bye."

The Moon's defence is that "the horrid old Kaiser" has taken advantage of her light and that she's being unfairly blamed, when the Sun and stars are not, yet they have also been shedding light on the Germans' nefarious acts. Britannia stops this squabbling but insists "we must do something to stop these intruders." In response, each fairy in turn offers to contribute to Britain's defence according to its magic powers: the Wind Fairy will blow mighty gales that push the pilots off course; the Snow Fairy will send blinding blizzards and Jack Frost will freeze the planes' petrol; the Wave Fairy will stir up mountainous waves, the Will of the Wisp will lure the German pilots to land in bogs and the Rain Fairy will send veils to hide the Moon. A song and a dance follow, in which the German planes' fate is depicted:

"This way my little Gothas steer,
And you will find your object near.
Come, trust our pretty wavering light
Or you'll be in a sorry plight.
Oh, nearer, nearer, come our way,
The guns they bark- ah! Well-a-day.
There! You've been hit on the side
Swamps will put an end to pride.
Little Gotha, now you fall
Round you dance the fairies small.
Down you sink and as you go
Hear the laughter, long and low,
Of Will of the Wisp, as he runs around
To lure fresh pilots to dangerous ground."

15

There's some concern that the rain will make mud for the troops at the front, but the Rain Fairy promises to keep the downpours away from the trenches and the Sun promises to dry out the ground in Flanders. Various patriotic declarations and a verse of 'God Save the King' follow.

Finally, the Will of the Wisp discovers Betty and Peggy asleep behind a bush. Britannia asks the fairies to carry them safely home as they are "only two of the myriads of children you must help me to protect." The fairies pick up the slumbering girls singing:

> "Fairy bells are ringing,
> 'Forward to the fray.'
> Fairy bands are mustering,
> Through the night and day.
> Fairy voices calling,
> 'Britain needs your aid,'
> Fairy echoes falling
> 'She shall be obeyed.'"

Then the short play ends with the fairies carrying the girls out in procession and singing a final stirring song:

> "Hear our Fairy ding-dong-bell.
> We who love our island well,
> When our foes approach our land,
> Marshal we our fairy band.
>
> Wave and Wind and Mist and Rain,
> Make the Gothas' journey vain.
> Britain, dear, we'll give to thee
> Lasting peace and victory."

Britain's Defenders is unlike any faery musical before or since, with its blood-thirsty and jingoistic tone. Many of the children who saw it must have felt baffled at how the delicate and peaceable fairies they knew from the books in their nurseries had turned into the vengeful sprites of the play. Even so, the violence, spite, and undisguised pleasure taken in the enemies' misfortune ought not to have shocked them, as the fairies of folk tradition (and many of the fairy tales of Grimm, Perrault and others) were just such cruel and vindictive creatures. Patry's faes are, in fact, some of the most authentic we shall meet- delighting in malignity for the sheer pleasure of doing ill to an adversary.

## Arnold Bax

Arnold Bax was a British composer for whom fairy and Celtic themes were of major significance during his early career. This stemmed from his time as a student at the Royal Academy of Music, between 1900 and 1905, during which Bax became greatly attracted to Ireland and Celtic folklore.

As a result of this Hibernian fascination, soon after his graduation, Bax departed from the classical influences he had learned and deliberately adopted what he conceived of as a 'Celtic' idiom. In 1908 he began a trilogy of tone poems called *Eire* (comprising *Into the Twilight*; *In the Faëry Hills* and *Ros Catha*) and, it seems, fully achieved his aims. Of *In the Faëry Hills*, a review in the *Manchester Guardian* said that "Mr Bax has happily suggested the appropriate atmosphere of mystery" and the *Musical Times* praised "a mystic glamour that could not fail to be felt by the listener."

## Bax's Influences

Bax's infatuation with Ireland must be set within the wider context of the *fin-de-siècle* decadence in which his youthful taste and imagination had developed. The Aesthetic fashion of the time favoured anything which was considered exotic enough to provide a pronounced contrast with the common-place concerns and ordinary practicalities of daily life. Theosophy, eastern mysticism, French Symbolist art and literature, and the spiritual view of the native Celtic world which prevailed (and was being promoted) at the time all contributed to the formation of Bax's taste and world view, whilst the influence of older cultural movements such as the Pre-Raphaelite medievalism of Rossetti and William Morris remained potent. There was much talk as well of neo-paganism and a strong interest in the occult, something intersecting in Ireland around W. B. Yeats. What's more, it seems certain that for a young person, a large part of the appeal of decadence and symbolism was their daring atmosphere of sexuality and freedom.

To these more general artistic influences can be added a number of specific musical developments. Bax will have absorbed, firstly, the daring novelties of Strauss, then, about a decade later, the lavish splendours of the Russian ballet, and, lastly and most importantly, the music drama of Wagner. From Wagner, the young composer would have learned that it was permissible to incorporate supernatural and mythical beings into his work, as well as acquiring what has been termed his "vague pantheism." Of course, Bax was not alone in these responses; he would have been encouraged, for example, by Granville Bantock's opera *Caedmar* (1892), and Hamish MacCunn's *Diarmid* (1897), both of which featured (respectively) elves, and gnomes and fairies, dancing.[5]

Bax was intoxicated with all of this romantic fantasy, but mystical Celticism in particular dominated his imagination for a time, leading directly to his fascination with Ireland. Even so, he remained equally susceptible to older poetry- to Keats, Shelley and, especially, to the work of Algernon Swinburne, who combined sex and paganism so thrillingly; he was also indebted to myth and folklore and to Russia, with its enthralling mix of Slavic folklore and Orthodox devotion. These were different aspects of the same extravagant imaginative ferment of the period, and they all left their mark on the young composer's music. Bax's brother, Clifford,

---

[5] K. B. Puffett, *Derrick Puffett on Music,* 2001, chapter 8, 'In the Garden of Fand: Arnold Bax & the Celtic Twilight,' 88.

described his sibling's early work as "Music fierce as fire, or hazed with unrelinquished/ Adolescent dreams of more than life can give."

W. B. Yeats was, of course, the high priest of the Celtic twilight and Bax duly fell under his spell. In 1902, as a "wide-eyed youth" of nineteen, he read Yeats' epic poem *The Wanderings of Oisin*, and "in a moment the Celt within me stood revealed."[6] In attempting to explain what he meant by this rhetorical phrase, Bax explained that (in his opinion) the 'Celt,' although he knew more clearly than most nationalities the difference between dreams and reality, deliberately chose to follow the dream. As he believed that there was "a tireless hunter of dreams" in his own make-up, Bax concluded that behind his everyday English exterior there existed an inner Celtic self. The fact that he had been able to recognise the true nature of this soul, Bax insisted, was a revelation he owed to Yeats. His was "the key that opened the gate of the Celtic wonderland to my wide-eyed youth," and it was shortly after this literary encounter with Niamh, Oisin, and enchanted islands in the western seas, that Bax visited Ireland for the first time.

Bax himself never expressed any doubt about what it was that Ireland had provided to him. If Yeats' particular brand of Irish Celticism allowed the young musician to bring his previously undirected adolescent emotions into some kind of aesthetic focus, and to recognise what he understood as his Celtic self, then the country provided him with a physical setting for that process. "My dream became localised," he said; the island embodied his imagination. Bax very evidently saw the country through an idealistic haze, creating a romantic image of a 'Celtic' race largely divorced from practical reality:

---

[6] Bax, *Farewell My Youth,* 1943, 41.

"I went to Ireland as a boy of nineteen in great spiritual excitement and once there my existence was at first so unrelated to material actualities that I find it difficult to remember it in any clarity. I do not think I saw men and women passing me on the roads as real figures of flesh and blood; I looked through them back to their archetypes, and even Dublin itself seemed peopled by gods and heroic shapes from the past."

He travelled extensively in the country and, for some years before the Great War, had homes both in England and in Ireland. He even wrote three volumes of Irish poetry under the pseudonym of Dermot O'Byrne. Bax's brother also lived in Dublin and through him the composer got to know the mystical poet and painter AE (William Russell) and so made contact with the Theosophists and their circle. In due course, Bax met Yeats; he later declared that the poet's work had more of an impact upon him than any music he had ever heard. Yeats not only wrote about the Irish faeries, the *sidhe* folk, (not just poetry but a folklore collection: *Fairy and Folk Tales of the Irish Peasantry,* 1888); he claimed to have met them as well.[7]

The result of this infatuation with the idea of Ireland can be heard in the music that Bax composed during this period. He recorded how the country seemed to be "bathed in supernal light":

"I worked very hard at the Irish language and steeped myself in history and saga, folk-tale and fairy-lore...Under this domination, my musical style became strengthened and purged of many alien elements. In part- at least- I rid myself of the sway of Wagner and Strauss and began to write Irishly, using figures and melodies of a definitely Celtic curve..."

Even so, Bax did not incorporate actual folk songs into his compositions. The Irish influence is clearest from the titles of

[7] Bax, *Farewell My Youth,* 48.

the overtures *A Connemara Revel* (1904) and *An Irish Overture* (1905), while the tone poem *Cathleen-ni-Hoolihan*, also of 1905, and the symphony *Into the Twilight* of 1908, clearly reflect his interest in Yeats' work. Despite his contact with, and sympathy for, the Gaelic-speaking population, Bax's music always belonged, nevertheless, to the "non-existent Ireland of the Celtic Twilight." This is expressed starkly in one of his descriptions of "the strange and wondrous sights to be seen in that wonderful country of the Wee Folks, of the Fairies." This is plainly not the reality of a poor British colony.

In fact, for his first important work, *A Celtic Song Cycle* of 1904, Bax chose to set poems by the Scottish writer Fiona Macleod (in fact Fiona Macleod was the Celtic *alter ego* of William Sharp, the Scottish critic, biographer and novelist). Macleod was, after Yeats, the greatest populariser of Celticism at the end of the nineteenth century, even though that writing is now virtually unknown. The composer produced about a dozen or so other songs to Macleod's verses over the subsequent few years. This poetry was arguably as much an inspiration for Bax during this decade as was the work of Yeats, although he never acknowledged this explicitly.

Fairy Music

Some of Bax's early work simply seeks to evoke a general 'Irish' or 'Celtic' mood by choosing suitable themes. For example, the symphony *Into the Twilight* began life as a sketch for an orchestral interlude in his projected opera, *Déirdre*, a work based on the life of the tragic Irish heroine. Only the opening measures of *Into the Twilight* were newly written in 1908; much of the rest of the score was simply a re-composition of one of his other student period works on a Celtic theme, *Cathleen-ni-Hoolihan*, which was written between 1903 and 1905 (and probably derived from Yeats' play of that name).

Supernatural themes soon started to come to the fore, however. Bax adapted William Allingham's well-known poem, *The Fairies,* as a song in 1908.[8] This was followed the next year by the symphonic poem *In the Faëry Hills*, to which the composer gave the alternative Irish title *An Sluagh Sidhe* (The Fairy Host). This work was directly inspired by Yeats' *The Wanderings of Oisin,* the poem that had made such an impression upon the teenaged Bax. He recorded the process of composition itself, describing how "I got this mood under Mount Brandon, with all W B [Yeats]'s magic about me- no credit to me of course, because I was possessed by [county] Kerry's self." Bax also wrote in a programme note for a performance of the work that he had sought "to suggest the revelries of the 'Hidden People' in the inmost deeps and hollow hills of Ireland".

In Yeats' *The Wanderings of Oisin* the fairy princess Niamh falls in love with the hero, Oisin, and his poetry and persuades him to join her on the immortal islands. He sings to the immortals what he conceives to be a song of joy, but his audience finds mere earthly joy intolerable:

> "But when I sang of human joy
> A sorrow wrapped each merry face,
> And, Patrick! by your beard, they wept,
> Until one came, a tearful boy;
> 'A sadder creature never stept
> Than this strange human bard," he cried;
> And caught the silver harp away'…"

The immortals then sweep Oisin into "a wild and sudden dance" that "mocked at Time and Fate and Chance".
The basic idea of a mortal being enticed away by supernatural forces is paralleled in another of Bax's orchestral works of the

---

[8] This famous verse has been set to music numerous times: for instance, by Henry Hadley (1894), Svein Sveinbjornsson (1890), Charles Villiers (1913), Reginald C. Robbins (1929) and by Crystal LaPoint Kowalski (1985).

same period, *The Garden of Fand* (1913-16).[9]  Bax recognised that the *sidhe* folk could be dangerous neighbours; he said that the music of *In the Faëry Hills* sought to evoke "an atmosphere of mystery and remoteness akin to the feeling with which the people of the West think of their beautiful and often terrible faeries".

## Pagan Music

Despite the importance of Yeats' mystical and fairy poetry to Bax's music, the composer's influences were much broader and deeper.  His works drew upon Irish and Arthurian myth, Scottish and Norse mythology, English folk tradition and classical Greek legends.  Indeed, Bax himself later scathingly dismissed the 'Celtic twilight' as "all bunk derived by English journalists from the spurious Ossian and the title of an early work by Yeats. Primitive Celtic colours are bright and jewelled."

The pagan Greek influence upon Bax was channelled through nineteenth century English literature such as Shelley's *Prometheus Unbound* and several poems by Algernon Swinburne, whose work was to displace that of Yeats' in its impact upon the young composer.  Swinburne's recreation of the ancient pagan world introduced a fresh element of ecstasy into English poetry- something which obviously had an enormous appeal for Bax, whose own youthful outpourings, both musical and literary, are notable for their intense passion.

Another of Bax's scores, *The Happy Forest* (1914), bears a title taken from a prose-poem by Herbert Farjeon which was itself influenced by the *Idylls* of Theocritus, a writer who is known as the 'father' of Greek pastoral poetry.  Bax used Farjeon as a point of departure for painting a musical

---

[9] Fand is also the subject of the second side of the 1977 concept album, *Aerie Faerie Nonsense,* released by *The Enid.*  Side one is based on Robert Browning's poem *Childe Roland to The Dark Tower Came*; it includes the track 'Ondine,' a mermaid or sea nymph.

impression of an enchanted wood filled with "the phantasmagoria of nature. Dryads, sylphs, fauns and satyrs abound- perhaps the goat-foot god may be there, but no man or woman."

The most important of Bax's scores from second decade of the century, *Spring Fire* (1913), was based largely on the first chorus of Algernon Swinburne's *Atalanta in Calydon*, quotations from which appear at the head of each movement in the score. Completed at Tintagel and published in 1865, Swinburne's poetic drama retells the Greek myth of the killing of the wild Calydonian boar by a band of heroes that includes the huntress Atalanta.

Bax felt himself drawn by the earthier, more primitive aspects of nature as they appear in Greek mythology. Thus, *Spring Fire* was an attempt, he wrote, to depict "'the first uprush and impulse of Spring in the woods." It is sensuous and sensual. In the section 'Daybreak' "The nymphs stretch their languid arms in the copses, and fauns and satyrs, and bizarre half-human shapes skip with mad antics down the deep glades. The sun rises on a glittering and dazzling earth." 'Woodland Love' follows, comprising "some strange harmony, as though the forest-lovers had become drugged with their own ecstatic dream." The piece concludes with 'Maenads,' which portrays the erotic adventures of sylvan demigods, the orgiastic frolics of Dionysian bacchantes and the followers of Pan and the ecstatic ceremonies concerned with the annual regeneration of nature. In his programme notes, Bax explained that the music in this section depicts "The dryads, maenads and bassarids [who] fly dancing and screaming through the woods, pursued relentlessly by Bacchus and Pan and their hordes of goat-footed and ivy-crowned revellers." He went on to describe how "Gradually elements from earlier parts of the composition become mingled into the thematic weft of this musical *Daphnephoria*. It is as though the whole of nature participated in the careless and restless riot of youth and sunlight." The Greek term Bax used means 'laurel-bearing' and refers to a Boeotian festival honouring Apollo, during which a laurel-decorated staff was carried in procession. Bax may have acquired the idea from J. G. Frazer's *The Golden Bough*, or he may have known Lord Leighton's 1876 painting *The Daphnephoria*. Whatever the source, it was fairly inappropriate, given that Leighton's scene is rather staid and respectable, as Victorian classicism so often is, and given the accepted contrast in the arts between Apollo (order) and Dionysus (unruly and emotional).[10]

Elemental phenomena- wild landscapes and seas- seem increasingly to have had a very powerful effect upon Bax. His friend, Mary Gleaves, recalled that the composer had an "almost erotic" empathy with trees, and there are sexual connotations to his sea music. Bax himself acknowledged the non-Celtic nature of the ideas behind *Spring Fire* and this other scores of the time and stated that "the true ecstasy of spring" and the "affirmation of life" are Hellenic concepts, foreign to the Celt: "Pan and Apollo, if ever they wandered so far from the Hesperidean garden as this icy Ierne [Ireland], were banished at once in a reek of blood and mist and fire…" The Celtic gods, the Irish heroes of myth and the faery tribe of the Tuatha De Danaan are noble and martial, but they may seem both too violent and yet distant. The classical nymphs and satyrs were hot blooded and vital: they spent their time in sunny glades, drinking and fornicating. Their attraction was much more immediate and apparent.

Bax's pagan scores date from the period just before the Great War, when there was a distinct artistic vogue for 'pagan' subjects. Nijinsky's production of *L'après-midi d'un faune* was first performed in Paris in 1912, and *The Rite of Spring* in 1913. Other works of the period are Ravel's *Daphnis et Chloé* (1910), and Skryabin's *Prometheus* (1913). Thus, in creating the finest of his pre-war compositions, Bax was not only

---

[10] See Nietzsche, *The Birth of Tragedy from the Spirit of Music,* 1872; Reynolds, *Shock & Awe,* 299; Leighton's canvas can be seen in the Lady Lever Art Gallery- it is full of matrons and their daughters singing, as if in church, all fully dressed and not in the least ecstatic.

embodying his own "adolescent dreams" but responding to a broader cultural trend. However, Bax's optimistic yearning for an imaginary Arcadian existence- what he later disparaged or dismissed as "the ivory tower of my youth" in 1949- was soon to be swept away by the harsh realities of the Great War, the Easter Rising in Ireland and, on a more personal level, the disintegration of his marriage. In his subsequent compositions, he never again visited the world of classical antiquity, nor tried to invoke the mystical excitement of his youth- but he did not forget those experiences either.[11]

## Nymphs & Faes

However short-lived the period of fae inspiration, we still have the Bax's pagan compositions. For example, *Nympholept* is a tone poem for solo piano, which was completed in July 1912. The title derives from Greek word *numpholēptos*, meaning one who suffers from nympholepsy, which in turn is the state of rapture inspired by nymphs.[12] On the manuscript score Bax wrote an explanatory note:

> "The tale telleth how one walking at summer-dawn in haunted woods was beguiled by the nymphs, and, meshed in their shining and perilous dances, was rapt away for ever into the sunlight life of the wild-wood."

It is, in essence, a poem about being 'taken by fairies.' Their dances are used to draw in, capture and abduct human males. Part of the lure, alongside simply joining the dance, is the desire of the men to get closer to the fairy girls- and hopefully have sex with one. Whether we're talking about Greek nymphs or British faes, the fundamental motivation is exactly the same- as is the peril that is concealed.

The title of Bax's work, meaning "captured by nymphs," was taken by him from an 1894 poem of the same name

---

[11] http://arnoldbax.com/the-pagan-world-of-arnold-bax-by-graham-parlett/.
[12] See my *Nymphology- A Brief History of Nymphs,* 2019.

by Algernon Swinburne, which "describes a "perilous pagan enchantment haunting the midsummer forest." In 1951, Bax also recorded that *Nympholept* was "based upon a poem… by Swinburne about panic induced by noonday silence in the woods."

The manuscript of the 1915 orchestral version of the work bears an additional note by Bax, a quotation from George Meredith's poem *The Woods of Westermain,* which conjures up images of the goddess, imps and enchantment:

> "Enter these enchanted woods/ You who dare…"

Bax himself also wrote a poem called *Nympholept*, which is dated 26th February 1912, five months before the piano score was completed. It was published anonymously in *Love Poems of a Musician* (London, 1923) and describes an encounter with a wood nymph or dryad:

> "… lifting brooding eyes, I found
> The woodland pied with primrose fire,
> The colours of new-born desire
> Flaunting in all the brakes around,
> While something skipped from the green ground.
>
> A thing born of wood-witcheries
> Happed delicately in flowers, with hair
> Blown wide and amber bosom bare,
> And pointed ears and slanted eyes
> Sharpening in quaint surprise.
>
> I stared.  She stared: then sudden flung
> Her brown chin up, and to the sky
> Jeered with an antic mirth, whilst I
> To mad-cap life was pricked and stung
> By the sweet taunting of her tongue.
>
> … Away she scampered, feigning fear,
> And her bare shoulder for my guide,

I chased all day the elfin bride.

And ere the dusk had dimmed the skies
I trapped her fast and learned this thing:
That demon birth of wanton Spring
With pointed ears and slanted eyes
Had surer wisdom than the wise."

Despite the classical title of the verse, it's highly arguable in fact that Bax's nymph far more closely resembles the archetypal faery of late Victorian and Edwardian British painting and literature than any Arcadian nymphet. Either way, she is sexy, naked and irresistible. Bax captures well the obsessive (and potentially dangerous) nature of passion for a fairy.

This poem- and his musical works- were not the products of mere fancy alone. The pianist Harriet Cohen performed many of his works and recorded this highly revealing conversation with Bax:

"He told us that when he really wished to concentrate he went up to a little village in the West Coast of Scotland because, there, he felt in touch with life mystical, with faeries, good and bad, and with all things that have made the fairy folk-lore of Scotland so famous.

Was it possible that this man honestly believed in faeries? Or had I misunderstood? Had Bax really seen Faeries? 'Yes' in Ireland. No doubt about it, he had definitely seen 'The Faeries'…

Arnold Bax was no uneducated country yokel with a deeply ingrained superstitious mind, but a man of culture and intellect swearing to a firm conviction of the supernatural. It is true that once, as a child, I thought I had seen a faery, and even today I am not prepared to say it was a figment of my imagination. She came dancing out of my mother's pet aspidistra. A lovely little person, like a Dresden china doll, with wings marked with a glittering phosphorescent substance, the colour of the rainbow, with flaxen hair, and skin like velvet. Rather hesitantly I told Arnold of my experience- at the same time waiting for the derisive hoots of laughter from my spouse. By this time, he was so intrigued by Arnold's stories, that he was quite prepared to accept even an Aspidistra faery to keep the family end up.

Arnold Bax did not laugh either- or merely politely accept my story as though I were trying to go 'one better'. Quite the reverse: he asked me for all the details, and said I was very lucky indeed to be blessed with the power to 'see', as it was seldom that a town dweller was privileged to meet any of the little people.

People, in the city, he said, had long since lost the art of seeing the faery-folk, although he assured me they were there, if only we had the eyes to see."

Bax's actual faery encounters seem to have come about through AE, William Russell (rather than Yeats). Russell claimed to be clairvoyant and, during a holiday the two friends took in Donegal, they had several faery encounters. One time, the pair were quietly reading, when Bax became suddenly aware of strange sounds around him, the like of which he had never heard before. He likened them to the mingling of rippling water and tiny bells tinkling- yet sufficiently clear in pitch that he could have written them down in musical notation. Russell asked if he could hear the music. Bax quietly confessed that he could, "and even as I spoke utter silence fell. I do not know what it was we both heard that morning and must be content to leave it at that." Almost certainly, the two men had heard the *ceol sidhe,* the faery music, a phenomenon widely recorded across Britain and Ireland.[13]

---

[13] See my *Faery,* 2020, chapter 8, 126-132.

On another occasion, at dusk, "many-coloured lights tossed and flickered along the ridges of the mountains. 'Don't you wish you were amongst them?' murmured Russell, and I knew he meant that we were gazing upon the host of fairy." Bax also witnessed "dancing shafts of flame (the wee folk?) and a white sword in a quivering circle of deep red." Another time, he saw "the silver fires of faerie twinkling all along the ridge and the tall phantoms dancing below us in the sand." He wrote to Yeats about the trip: "The gods have returned to Erin and have centred themselves in the sacred mountains and blow the fires through the country... The bells are heard from the mounds and sound in the hollows of the mountains. A purple sheen in the inner air, perceptible at times in the light of day, spreads itself over the mountains."

Reflecting on these experiences in later life, Bax was still prepared to confide that he really did believe in the physical reality of fairies.

## John Ireland

For Arnold Bax, the love of myth and fairy lore was initially an intellectual and literary matter, but the fascination was later reinforced by experience. Remarkably, the situation was exactly the same for fellow British composer John Ireland. Reading strengthened his interest in the mystical, which later found confirmation in personal experience. He once made this unequivocal declaration about himself: "I am a Pagan. A Pagan I was born and a Pagan I shall remain- that is the foundation of religion."[14]

## The Influence of Arthur Machen

Just as Bax was 'awoken' by Yeats and MacLeod, the key factor in Ireland's philosophy and music was the writing of the Welsh novelist, Arthur Machen. The composer first came

---

[14] Lewis Foreman (ed.), *The John Ireland Companion*, 2011, c.10.

across the author's work when he picked up a copy of *The House of Souls* at Preston railway station in 1906. He said that the cover attracted him to buy the book without hesitation and, upon starting to read, he had instantly loved it. Ireland claimed that the book's impact upon him was as important as had been that of reading De Quincey's *Confessions of an Opium Eater.* Putting Machen on a par with De Quincey is a considerable compliment.[15]

Nearly thirty years after buying *The House of Souls,* Ireland was to get to know Machen personally, staying at his home a couple of times, but the author's world of fantasy and mystery had an immediate effect upon him. Machen's books have been described as a "catalyst" for the musician, something which "infused" his compositions. He himself went so far as to declare that his music could not be understood unless the listener had also read Machen's stories.

Ireland elevated Machen to the status of a "seer." The composer's interest in magic and the unknown were ignited by what Machen portrayed and he came to share with the author a belief in the subconscious or 'racial memory'- the idea that through ancient sites such as barrows and standing stones one could connect to ancient pagan ceremonies and to druidic mysticism. At Chanctonbury Ring and Maiden Castle hillforts, for example, Ireland believed that he could still detect the early rites that had been performed there.

Ireland was especially fascinated by magic, rituals and by the occult. He shared this, too, with Machen, who was a member of the Golden Dawn along with W. B. Yeats, Aleister Crowley, Bram Stoker and fellow fantasy novelist Algernon Blackwood. Ireland's particular devotion was to Pan (something he shared with his contemporary Sir Granville Bantock who kept a statue on his piano). In 1952 he lamented that:

---

[15] John Longmore, *John Ireland- Portrait of a Friend,* 1969, 4 & 20.

"The Great God Pan has departed from this planet, driven hence by the mastery of the material and the machine over mankind."

Ireland's views as to the cult of Pan may reflect the apparent waning of the Edwardian interest in the god. Nevertheless, his overall philosophical and religious position was clearly mystical, spiritual and anti-materialist. He was open to the supernatural and the inexplicable.[16]

Arthur Machen was not, of course, John Ireland's sole influence. He drew musically upon the spirit of Stravinsky's *Rite of Spring* and he also found John Brand's *Observations on Popular Antiquities,* a rich source of English fairy lore and folk tradition, an inspiration. The fairy author, Sylvia Townsend Warner, who happened also to be a relative of Machen, was a further influence, her concerns with physical and mental ecstasy matching Ireland's own.

The Hill of Dreams

Ireland found Machen's major novel *The Hill of Dreams* (1907) highly compelling and reckoned that it deserved a place in the 'literary hierarchy.' It never ceased to be a source of inspiration for him.[17]

The book is the strange and at times trance-like story of a young man, Lucian, who seems to come into contact with an ancient cult within an overgrown hill fort- "fairy bulwarks" as he terms the site- near his home. He is unable to forget (nor to escape) the experience, nor can he fully release himself from an early infatuation with a local girl who seems to be able to speak a strange faery tongue. Lucian comes to suspect that he himself is descended from 'the little people,' wondering whether "there were some drop of fairy blood in his body that

---

[16] Fiona Richards, *The Music of John Ireland*, 2000, 66; on Pan, see my *Great God Pan*, 2021.
[17] Fiona Richards, *The Music of John Ireland,* 2000, 63, 64 & 66.

made him foreign and strange to the world." For the young man, the whole of the area around his home near Caerleon becomes a fairyland, whilst he regards himself as a 'changeling,' increasingly alienated from the society and conventions of the material world around him. He tries to become a writer, but the boundaries between his imagination and daily life seem to dissolve until it is very unclear what he has experienced and what he has dreamed. Eventually, therefore, Lucian returns to the hill fort and is reclaimed in an orgiastic rite by the satyrs and witches, who are led by his former girlfriend- transformed into a terrifying priestess. He is overwhelmed by the black magic and by the seductive "wood whisper" of the fauns.

Machen's book probably helped shape Ireland's piano concerto, *Mai-Dun,* which takes its title from the name Thomas Hardy used in his Wessex novels for Maiden Castle. However, like Machen, Ireland probably saw the ancient site not so much as an Iron Age monument but as a "faery rath" just like that which obsessed Lucian.[18]

The White People

One of the two stories in Machen's *House of Souls* is the remarkable *White People,* a curious stream-of-consciousness account by a young girl of her encounters with mysterious and beautiful White People. As a little girl she sees these beings emerge from a pond to dance and sing. When she is older, she also becomes involved in a secret cult, discovers a lost altar to Pan, and has revealed to her the hidden mysteries of the water nymphs. The exact identity of the supernatural beings she encounters- whether or not they are faeries in a traditional sense- is not revealed. There is some suggestion that humans can transform into White People (this appears to happen to the girl's nurse) whilst the nymphs are definitely aquatic, are differentiated by colour and have magical powers. We are informed by the girl that she was instructed by her

---

[18] M. Searle, *John Ireland- The Man and His Music,* 1979, 30, 34, 44 & 85.

nurse in "the old words of the fairy language" as a protection against being taken by them.

Ireland declared that this haunting story had "astounding qualities" at which he "never ceased to marvel." He is correct; it is a unique and breathless narrative by the girl, full of suggestive ideas that we are left to muse upon ourselves: for example, Machen leaves undefined not only the nature of the Nymphs, but also the identity of "the Dôls, or Jeelo, or what voolas mean," who or what is "the Alala," what exactly is "the way to make the Aklo letters, or the Chian language." We hear of the Xu, with their little white faces, who came to speak to the child when she was still in her cradle, but learn no more about them. The story is full of hints of tantalising mysteries that are deliberately left enigmatic; there is a mood of threat, danger and persecution, but none of these are ever clarified.

Machen's novella directly inspired three very short piano suites written in 1913 by Ireland, *Island Spell, Moon-Glade* and *Scarlet Ceremonies,* which he grouped together under the title *Decorations*. *Scarlet Ceremonies* took its title directly from *The White People.* Two of its movements are headed by citations from poet Arthur Symons; for example, *Island Spell* begins:

"I would wash the dust of the world in a soft green flood,
Here, between sea and sea in the fairy wood,
I have found a delicate, wave-green solitude…"

As we'll see again later, the Islands of the Green Flood are the vanishing faery isles in the Irish Sea off the west coast of Wales.

The third song of Ireland's *Scarlet Ceremonies* borrows from directly Machen's text:

"Then there are the ceremonies, which are all of them important, but some are more delightful than others: there are White Ceremonies, and the Green

34

Ceremonies, and the Scarlet Ceremonies. The Scarlet Ceremonies are the best..."

Yet again, Machen left these rites undefined- and all the more intriguing for being so.

Ireland's fascination with pagan ritual is also demonstrated by 1913's brief prelude for orchestra, *Forgotten Rite,* a composition that has been said to be permeated with Machen's notion of a "world beyond the walls," and with the proximity of the supernatural. *Rite* was particularly inspired by the ancient megalithic landscapes of the Channel Islands, places that Ireland described as being especially 'Machenish.' It is also consciously evocative of Pan, with flutes imitating the panpipes.

Early in 1940, Ireland was living on Guernsey. His home at l'Erée Bay was situated just below one of the island's most important burial mounds, *Creux ès Faies* ('the faery hollows). In *Sarnia* (1940) Ireland pursued this theme, celebrating the ecstasy of communing with nature. This 'Island Sequence' comprises three piano pieces, 'Le Catioroc' (a headland crowned by the impressive *Le Trepied* dolmen), 'In a May Morning' and 'Song of the Springtides,' the latter prefaced by a quotation from Swinburne. The ritualistic mood again derives from Machen's novel *The Great God Pan.*

We might also suspect that Ireland's interests in Pan and paganism led to his decision to compose an overture based upon Petronius' *Satyricon* in 1946. Ireland admitted to being greatly attracted by the "general atmosphere of roguery and vagabondage" pervading the text; to be frank, debauched sexuality might be a better term: there are gay relationships, sexual torture, the consumption of aphrodisiacs and the deflowering of a seven-year-old girl. The score itself, though, composed at the request of Henry Wood for a Promenade concert, is perfectly mild.

In 1933 John Ireland was visiting the South Downs in Sussex. He was working on a new composition and set out alone early one morning to walk high up on top of the Downs near Arundel so as to visit a ruined chapel called Friday's Church at Harrow Hill.

Arriving at the site, Ireland was irritated to find that he was not alone, despite the early hour. A group of children dressed in white appeared near him and started to dance. He watched them for some time before it began to dawn upon him that the infants themselves made no sound and that their feet upon the turf were silent. He looked away, briefly distracted, and when he turned back- they had vanished.

Ireland was convinced that he had had a fairy experience- and the incident definitely has all the hallmarks of an authentic faery contact: the individuals he saw were of child stature, they were engaged in dancing outdoors, yet were at the same time slightly detached from the material world, and, lastly, a moment's inattention broke the spell and allowed them to vanish.

The composer wrote in detail about this incident to Machen, whose laconic reply was:

"Oh, so you've seen them too?"

Ireland's piano concerto *Legend* (1933) was the product of this experience.

## Edward Elgar and the *real* Starlight Express

We are all familiar with Andrew Lloyd Webber's musical, *Starlight Express*; the truth is, though, that its title was not original: it was borrowed from a 1915 composition by Sir Edward Elgar.

Fantasy and horror writer Algernon Blackwood, who has several faery short stories to his name, wrote a novel for younger readers in 1913- *A Prisoner in Fairyland*. The text was adapted into a play for children by Violet Alice Pearn and, in due course, the idea arose to create a musical from the stage play, as a "piece of Red Cross work for the mind during the first agony of the war." Sir Edward Elgar, the distinguished classical composer, was approached to provide the songs and incidental music.

The choice of Elgar may, at first glance, seem surprising, but he was in fact a very suitable choice. At the age of eleven, he had written a musical play- to be performed by his brother and sisters- which would become the two *The Wand of Youth* suites, four decades later, in 1907. The composer described the childish piece in these terms. It contrasted youth and age, being set in a world from which adults were excluded:

"Some small grievances occasioned by the imaginary despotic rule of my father and mother (the 'Two Old People' of the text) led to the devising of the [original] *Wand of Youth*. By means of a stage allegory- which was never wholly completed- it was proposed to show that children were not properly understood.

The scene was a Woodland Glade, intersected by a brook; the hither side of this was our fairyland; beyond, small and distant, was the ordinary life which we forgot as often as possible. The characters on crossing the stream, entered fairyland and were transfigured. The Old People were lured over the bridge by the 'Moths and Butterflies' and the 'Little Bells;' but these devices did not please; the Old People were restive and failed to develop that fairy feeling necessary for their well-being. While fresh devices were making, 'The Fairy Pipers' charmed them to sleep; this sleep was accompanied by 'The Slumber Scene.' To awaken the Old People glittering lights were flashed in their eyes by means of 'Sun

37

Dance.' Other episodes- 'The Fountain Dance' etc.- whose character can be deduced from the titles- followed, and the whole concluded with the 'March'."[19]

In Elgar's youthful fairyland, the 'Two Old People' are woken from their mystical sleep by dancing fairies and lights to discover that they have been transported back to their childhoods and have been filled with youthful wisdom, realising that living in Faery is preferable to life in the 'real' world.

The first suite of the mature *Wand of Youth* is divided into several sections. In 'Fairy Pipers' the stage direction states that "Two fairy pipers pass in a boat, and charm them to sleep," an authentic notion of the enchanting quality of faery music. The final scene is titled 'Fairies and Giants,' which Elgar derived from a *Humoreske* dated 1867. He later reused it again in *Starlight Express*.

For *A Prisoner in Fairyland*, Elgar worked to a very short timescale. He was asked to compose the score on November 11th 1915 and, by recycling the ideas from his youth, he had the music ready for rehearsals at the start of December. The production opened at the Kingsway Theatre in London on December 29th. Whilst the music was praised, the adaptation of the book was *not* regarded as a success by critics- although the target audience of children seemed to enjoy it- and so the production ran for only forty performances over just one month. There were problems with the staging and with the loss of key personnel: both the original composer and the intended producer were called up for military service and Elgar himself was unable to conduct when his wife had a car accident days before the opening night. The main problem, though, was the script. Blackwood complained at "this murder of my simple little play. Arts and Crafts pretentious rubbish stitched onto your music by a silly crank who has never read

---

[19] Ian Parrott, *Elgar*, 1977, 57.

the play." The play's sentimental mysticism seemed to the taste of very few.

It seems that Blackwood was not being entirely frank with Elgar when he sought to shift the blame like this. Blackwood and Pearn, the latter being the winner of the *Era*'s 1913 Playwrights' Competition for *The Minotaur*, had in fact begun working together on the adaptation of *The Prisoner of Fairyland* soon after its publication in 1913 and had sought interest from several theatre managements for its production. In fact, Pearn proved to be a prolific dramatist who actually went on to adapt several other of Blackwood's works, including *Karma- A Reincarnation Play* in 1918. Admittedly, though, she was still something of a novice in 1915, being only twenty-five years of age.

The plot of the hour-long performance is slender indeed. The general idea is that, in time of war, only children can provide comfort and restore unity. Conflict was represented by a troubled family whose children form a secret society and identify themselves with the constellations. They live in 'star caves' and their mission is to restore harmony to the "wumbled" (worried and muddled) adults by means of sprinklings of star dust. As one song puts it:

> "Kiss me again 'til I sleep and dream
> That I'm lost in your fairylands…
> For the grown-up folk are troublesome folk
> And the book of their childhood is torn,
> Is blotted and crumpled and torn!"

Sprites descend from the starlight express and scatter their star dust, crying:

> "Unwumble deftly! The world has need of you!
> They'll listen to my song and understand
> That exiled over long from fairyland,
> The weary world has rather lost its way."

The fairy plan is to sow earth's "little gardens of unrest" with joy and trust, thereby to restore "Love, laughter, courage, hope."

We considered earlier *Britain's Defenders*. Along with that and a third Great War fae play, *The War Fairies, The Starlight Express* explores much of the same territory- the function that children and fairies may perform in restoring peace and harmony to a riven society- albeit with less direct interventions in human affairs by the Good Folk than are seen in the two other productions.

The play's failure consigned it to obscurity (although Elgar's score is still performed and recorded) and this enabled Lloyd Webber to purloin the title without any fear of confusion. Nevertheless, it is another fascinating little document attesting the role of fairies during wartime in the early twentieth century.

## Rutland Boughton

My consideration of early twentieth century British music and the impact upon it of visions of Faery concludes with an examination of the work of Rutland Boughton. He may be unknown to almost all readers, but he's a fascinating subject for many reasons- for his fae operas, for his radical political views and because he was the founder of the original Glastonbury festival. Boughton has been described as a "socialist, patriot, musician and domestic genius, an agnostic of deep religious feeling and a man of many contradictory characteristics."

Boughton was born in Aylesbury in 1878. His family ran a grocer's shop which was not particularly successful, meaning that his schooling and prospects were limited. However, through luck and hard work, he managed to establish the musical career he had aspired to and, by the early 1900s, he was developing a reputation as a teacher and composer. He was working in Birmingham and his experience there with choirs convinced him of "the immense civilising influence of music and he began to feel that music, and art generally, might one day succeed where religion had failed." Boughton pursued these thoughts in a book, *Music Drama of the Future,* in 1911. He had become aware of:

> "the truly popular nature of all the greatest art and of the fact that the greatest artists acquire their superhuman power by acting as the expression of the 'oversoul' of a people."

Like Bax, Boughton was a great admirer of Wagner and argued that he had chosen folk subjects for his operas (such as the *Rheingold*) because these myths had been produced by this 'oversoul.'

## British Legend and British Drama

*Music Drama of the Future* formed a sort of manifesto for Boughton. He wanted to produce heroic music dramas based upon the British 'national scriptures'- stories like the legends of King Arthur- which he regarded as the birth right of the British people. In addition, the young composer wanted to create a national theatre within which this musical project might be realised and which might, in turn, lie at the heart of a larger community. He argued that previous attempts at communes had failed because they lacked a religious centre- a function the theatre could perform. He realised that he needed to find a "civically conscious" place where he could co-operate with the inhabitants to develop a "new city" focused on the drama venue.

Around this time too, Boughton began to collaborate with writer Reginald Buckley. They shared a mutual love of Wagner, Ruskin, Milton, Dante and Tennyson and each wanted to write 'music drama.' Buckley had already written a text called *Arthur of Britain* and had been searching for a composer to produce a score. Boughton had already identified the Arthurian myths as a subject. He saw them as the "best tap into the mystical heart of Great Britain."

A Social Experiment

There were various false starts in the plan for establishing the national theatre. Boughton proposed a summer school at Hindhead in 1912 and then went on to consider Letchworth Garden City as a possible setting for his experiment. By 1913, however, he'd chosen Glastonbury in Somerset as the best location in which to found his "English Bayreuth" and had moved into a large house called Chalice Well where he also opened a school of music and drama. The aim of this institution was to train local singers, instrumentalists and dancers so that they could perform in his planned festivals, which would take place four times a year, at Easter, Whitsuntide, August and at Christmas.

Boughton's plans were ambitious and unusual: he envisaged a festival linked to a commune for artists who preferred a country life and who felt that they should earn their livings through art combined with running a co-operative farm. In 1916 he wrote that "the whole business is for me as much a sociological as an aesthetic thing." He and Buckley wanted to control the performances of their works completely, but they also wanted to involve the local community actively in all aspects of the festivals- performing, designing clothes and scenery and choreographing dances.

Boughton was evidently ahead of his time- and not just artistically. This fact was demonstrated by his unconventional love life. He had married in 1903, but the marriage had not been wise or successful. Whilst in Birmingham he had formed a relationship with a music lover called Christine Walshe and in 1911 Boughton left his wife and moved in with Christina.

The first *Glastonbury Festival of Music Drama and Mystic Drama* opened inauspiciously on August 5th 1914- the day after Britain entered the First World War. It featured performances of 'A Chapel in Lyonesse,' which was based on a poem by William Morris, and the *Immortal Hour,* based on the faery play of that name by Scottish poet Fiona Macleod (you may recall that Arnold Bax also drew inspiration from Macleod's work).

We'll discuss this opera in more detail later, but it proved to be extremely popular and has been called "England's greatest fairy opera." The *Immortal Hour* was performed again at Easter 1915 and again in August 1916. That summer saw the first performance too of Boughton and Buckley's Arthurian opera *The Round Table.*

'Music of the Duration'

Despite the war, the Glastonbury Festival continued in 1915 and the following year. However, just as the 1916 Festival ended, Boughton received his call-up papers from the Army. He appealed this to a tribunal, on the grounds that his musical and educational work in Glastonbury was "of national importance." In this he may have found encouragement from Lloyd George who, in 1916, had asked "Why should we not sing during the war?" He had been speaking in support for the annual Welsh *eisteddfod* but Boughton might well have drawn a parallel with his own English venture.

The authorities, though, did not accept Boughton's case- even though he argued that the Glastonbury festivals could draw money away from Bayreuth and Oberammergau- and for the next two years the festival was suspended whilst he served King and country. It has to be admitted, as well, that whilst other artists like Tolkien, Ledwidge or Graves served on the front line, Boughton never did. He was bandmaster of a succession of regiments. Nevertheless, when in December 1918 *The Times* newspaper reviewed the music composed during the war, it recognised Boughton's contribution.

As soon as the war was over, Boughton began planning the revival of the festival.  He moved to a new and larger house in Glastonbury, called Mount Avalon, which served as a school and hostel and at the first post-war festival, in August 1920, he presented *The Immortal Hour, The Round Table* and the new opera written with Buckley, *The Birth of Arthur.*

The revived festival as an idea, and the individual performances, attracted great praise and encouragement, but there was, too, a universal feeling that it could not grow as it should so long as the main venue was the cramped Assembly Rooms in the High Street, in which there was neither space for larger audiences nor for the performers.  Nonetheless, there were great hopes for the future and admiration for the way all the performers were able to contribute- as well as to develop their skills.  *The Times* had, for example, been impressed how the school's teachers had "discovered the children of the town to be fairies, nymphs, water sprites and elves."

The festival continued until 1927 but steadily declined, despite successful national tours.  A major contributing factor in this loss of popular support was Boughton's 'adulterous' circumstances- combined with his left-wing opinions.  In 1923 he separated from Christina and moved in with one of his local pupils, a woman called Kathleen.  This was scandalous in the Glastonbury of the 1920s- pupils were withdrawn from the schools by their parents and money was withheld for developing a dedicated theatre in the town.  Money, in any case, had always been a problem: the festival launched with appeals for funds and always made a loss.  Eventually the festival company went into liquidation; nevertheless, it had presented 350 stage performances and 100 concerts during its existence and permanently had an effect on the little town of Glastonbury.

In November 1927 Boughton moved to a smallholding at Kilcot on the edge of the Forest of Dean in Gloucestershire, where he and Kathleen raised a family, kept pigs, goats and hens and grew vegetables and cider apples. From this point on, his career also sank steadily into obscurity- something he ascribed (perhaps with a hint of paranoia) to his political views.

## Politics

During the early 1920s Boughton was involved with the London Labour Choral Union. Along with Labour politician Herbert Morrison, he believed that "working class music making could be an invigorating element in Socialist politics and culture." The choral union was indeed a vital part of Labour Party culture until it was cut as an unaffordable luxury.

Before then, though, Boughton had joined the Communist Party, expressing his belief in organised control by the workers. He identified personally with this, because he felt that, as a composer, he had very little control over the fruits of his labour. Boughton resigned from the Party in 1929, complaining that he felt he had been undervalued and underused, but re-joined in 1945, only to quit again in 1956 over the invasion of Hungary.

It was only very late in his life that Boughton returned to the Arthurian Cycle, which he had largely abandoned after the death of Buckley in 1919. He wrote the final two operas, *Galahad* and *Avalon,* in the mid-1940s. The final scene of *Avalon* shows his continuing belief in Socialist principles: the Lady of the Lake reveals three visions of past, present and future to the dying King Arthur. These are the star of Bethlehem, the white star of hope shining over his own land and, finally, a red star that will rise in the east. At the outset, Boughton had seen Arthur as "an essentially British fount of inspiration," but clearly over the decades the vision changed from Wagnerian epic to a political tract with strong religious overtones. The cycle as a whole may not be an aesthetic or musical success, but it has been described as "an extraordinary demonstration of artistic courage and determination- a ruin perhaps, but undeniably impressive."

Certainly, the Arthurian Cycle to many seemed to represent the *raison d'etre* of a national festival founded in Avalon; the dramas were the source of the festival's vitality and its justification. Arthur could only truly be celebrated in the town where he had (allegedly) been buried with his queen.

## Faeryland

As will be apparent, myth and faerie magic suffuse much of Boughton's work. They are of course present in the Arthurian cycle, but he also wrote a range of other songs and operas based on fairy poems. These include *Faery People* by Mary Webb and a large number of poems by Fiona Macleod, amongst which are *Dalua* and *Avalon,* part of Boughton's *Six Celtic Choruses.*

The most important of these latter works is *The Immortal Hour.* Christina Walshe was very influential in developing Boughton's taste for Irish and Scottish mythology. She was half Irish and was a great supporter of the 'Celtic revival.' Boughton studied Hebridean folk songs before writing the music for *The Hour* and, whilst he was absent in the army in September 1918, she arranged performances of W. B. Yeats' play *The Land of Heart's Desire* alongside a production of *The Immortal Hour.*

Fiona Macleod wrote a great deal of mystical and mythical poetry, amongst which are a small number of verses with an explicit fairy theme, including *The Bugles of Dreamland, The Hills of Ruel, The Moon Child, The Lords of Shadow, Dreams Within Dreams* and *The Last Fay. The Immortal Hour* is a dramatic poem of some seventy pages concerned with Celtic myth and the *sith* folk.

Macleod's *Immortal Hour* has been described as being ideal for Boughton as it was "a legend only half told, with meanings hinted at, never spoken out." This left him free to mould the work into any musical shape that appealed. He did so, but still left much to the audience's imaginations. As *The Times* acknowledged in 1919, "the vague imagery of Fiona Macleod was easy to catch in music- and easy to dissipate." Boughton had captured it effectively. Whilst the original play was "visionary and vague" the opera was visionary but not vague and was full of haunting tunes.

Macleod's play is very short- only two brief acts- and not a great deal happens in it. In the first act, the fairy princess Etain and High King of Ireland, Eochaid, are brought together as lovers by fairy trickster Dalua. In the second act Etain's former lover, Midir, comes from Faery in search of her. She remembers her former life and departs with Midir whilst Dalua casts a spell of death over Eochaid. The drama is perhaps best known for the recurring 'fairy song':

> "How beautiful they are, the lordly ones,
> who dwell in the hills, in the hollow hills."

We shall encounter these words again later, when a new genre of British music took up faery themes.

## Modern Classical Music

Faery has not been entirely forgotten by classical music in more recent decades, but (as in rock) Tolkien's *Lord of the Rings* has had a possibly disproportionate influence upon composers.

In 1967, the Welsh musician, composer and singer Donald Swann wrote the song cycle *The Road Goes Ever On*, which contained initially six of Tolkien's songs from *Lord of the Rings* (another three were added subsequently). Swann had already demonstrated his interest in 'fantasy' themes with an opera based upon C. S. Lewis' science fiction story *Perelandra*. For the *Road Goes Ever On,* Swann collaborated with Tolkien, the Quenya song '*Namárië*' being set to a melody resembling a Gregorian chant which Tolkien had hummed to Swann after hearing a performance of the first draft of the cycle. Besides this musical input, the author also provided decorations in elvish script for each page of the published sheet music version, the Sindarin prayer '*A Elbereth Gilthoniel*' with a guide to the grammar of the language and notes on the First Age of Middle Earth.

In 1988, the Dutch composer and trombonist Johan de Meij completed his Symphony No.1, *The Lord of the Rings*. The work comprises five movements, which are titled, sequentially, 'Gandalf,' 'Lothlórien,' 'Gollum,' 'Journey in the Dark' (which is in turn made up of two parts, 'The Mines of Moria' and 'The Bridge of Khazad-Dûm') and 'Hobbits.' The piece has been widely performed and recorded during the subsequent decades.

Norwegian neo-classical composer Martin Romberg has written three full-scale symphonic poems for orchestra, *Quendi* (2008), *Telperion and Laurelin* (2014), and *Fëanor* (2017), all of which are inspired by passages from *The Silmarillion*. Romberg has called his work 'fantasy music' and he has argued for the fresh vitality that various mythologies can bring to classical scores. He has also composed two piano pieces based upon *The Silmarillion- Valaquenta* (2009) and *Earendil* (2013)- and a choral work, *Eldarinwë Líri* using elvish poems (2009-10). In addition, Romberg has composed scores influenced by the Norse *Havamal,* by Irish myth, by various world mythologies and by the poems written by fantasy horror author H. P. Lovecraft.

Lastly, Howard Shore's soundtracks to the six Peter Jackson films based upon *Lord of the Rings* and *The Hobbit* have come to be recognised as popular classical works in their own right.

## Popular Music

People have always sung about the faeries, as well as telling each other folktales concerning them.  As a result, one major source of information on traditional faery beliefs is the body of late medieval and early modern ballads that have survived.  I have described these separately in my *Faery Ballads and Rhymes* (2019).

Ballads were the popular songs of Britain.  They were composed at unknown times, in unknown places, by people who are now completely anonymous to us, but they were preserved for centuries by ordinary folk, who memorised, performed and passed them on and, by so doing, made them part of the national culture.  Ballads are narrative songs, telling notable stories in a memorable form.  As such, they have provided another route by which folktales and fairy lore have been transmitted from generation to generation.  Barely a dozen fairy ballads exist, but some of them are amongst the best-known songs of all.  These include 'Allison Gross, 'Clerk Colvill,' 'Tam Lin,' 'The Wee Wee Man' and 'Leesom Brand.'  We'll encounter some of them again later, too.

### Ballad Development

There are broadly two types of ballad: the 'traditional ballad,' the product of a pre-literate rural community which is reflective of many very old beliefs and ceremonies, and the 'urban ballad,' the product of a growing urban population of literate or semi-literate consumers.

The earliest ballads derive from a variety of sources, from medieval minstrels' lays, from dance songs, and from the medieval knightly romances.  Some of the traditional ballads incorporate elements from very ancient myths and folktales, some come from Arthurian legend and some are historical and are taken from the chronicles.[20]  These songs were originally composed to entertain noble households, but subsequently they were transmitted orally within communities, making them as much 'folk music' as any of the more traditional folksongs. The earliest 'traditional ballads' we possess come from the late fourteenth century. Most are of fifteenth and sixteenth century date, but none have been left untouched by later generations. Their transmission through live performance has inevitably led to their transformation and development; singers changed them to suit their own tastes as well as to respond to current events and audience demands.

The majority of the 'urban' or 'street' ballads have survived as printed broadsides. These first began to appear in the early sixteenth century, typically being composed and hawked in the public places in response to the latest events and news. That said, there was still a market for new editions of the older, traditional ballads. Equally, new lyrics were often paired with existing and familiar tunes. The production of urban ballads really took off in the seventeenth century and then continued well into the mid-nineteenth century, when newspapers and music hall both began to displace them. By this time, they were being published not just in London but in most of the major cities of England.

Ballads are typified by being short dramatic narratives, generally composed of short stanzas, with a high proportion of dialogue to description, commentary and moralisation. Hand in hand with this, ballads can be quite amoral: they are not intended to be improving- just entertaining. Sex and violence are common. Ballads are meant to be sung and have a distinct style, a common feature being their choruses or refrains, phrases that are repeated throughout. As for their content, the earliest examples of the type are rich in folklore and make much use of dwarf kings, ghosts and other wicked spirits, elves and fairies, taboos, dark magic and enchantments and marvels.

---

[20] G. Gregory Smith, *The Transition Period- European Literature of the Fifteenth Century,* 1900.

Whilst ballads steadily declined in popularity from the end of the seventeenth century, they took a century and a half to fall entirely from favour and, in that time, they experienced something of a creative revival.

Many of the early folklorists who collected ballads were also poets (amateur as well as professional) and a vogue arose- particularly in Scotland- for the composition of 'modern ballads.' Written in Scots, often by individuals with strong rural roots, these songs can frequently be quite hard to distinguish from the sixteenth century originals. These works were well furnished with elves and fairies dancing in moonlight, as well as featuring creatures such as brownies and kelpies.

This two-way traffic between the 'high art' of literature and the popular art of ballads was nothing new. As has already been described, the ballads grew out of the courtly romances of the Middle Ages and the early modern period saw continued borrowings and inspiration. Shakespeare quoted from the story of *Child Rowland* in *King Lear;* his treatment of Puck was fed back into broadsheet stories of Robin Good-fellow's life. The plot of *Child Rowland* was also used by John Milton for his masque *Comus* whilst a song from the libretto of Henry Purcell's short opera, *The Fairy Queen,* which was mentioned earlier, was pirated as a broadside lyric.

When, in 1843, many of the statutory restrictions formerly imposed upon musical theatre by the Lord Chamberlain were relaxed, it led to an explosion in popular entertainment in the form of music halls and, later, pantomimes. This, and the repeal of stamp duty upon newspapers- which permitted a huge expansion in their publication- together marked the end of the active commercial life of ballads. Their musical role was inherited in many respects by light entertainment in theatres. In the later Victorian period, this is where fairy songs were being written and performed. Gilbert and Sullivan are the best-known composers in this genre, but there were very many pantomimes and operettas that depended upon Faery and magic for their drama and visual interest; another, late example, is Seymour Hicks' *Bluebell in Fairyland,* described earlier. Here, too, we reconnect with the more 'highbrow' music discussed in the first chapter.

## Music Hall

Existing in a space between folk songs, nursery rhymes, and the slightly higher brow light opera of Gilbert and Sullivan, was British popular theatre. In late Victorian times, music hall and (especially) pantomime brought faeries onto the stage and played a leading role in shaping public perceptions of the appearance of faery kind and their typical behaviour. Pantomimes had a leading role in this, not least through the manner of these performances' staging. Productions such as *Tom Thumb* (a character derived from a ballad), the *Merry Pranks of the Good Little People* and the *Doomed Princess of the Fairy Hall* (not to mention perennial fairy tale favourites like *Goldilocks*) were all enlivened by gas lighting, lime light, scenery and stage effects during what was the first great age of British pantomime. These productions increasingly involved spectacular 'transformation scenes' in which characters or scenery changed before the audience's eyes. In due course, such magical extravaganzas became central to performances and, by the end of the century, the standard end to any pantomime was the revealing of fairy land ('the realms of bliss') in which fairies would appear and vanish through trap doors and would fly across the stage. Mention should also be made of faery entertainment in the form of popular freak-shows, which offered the paying public dwarves, changelings and displays of magic- for example, the *World of Spirits* and *Phantoms of the Witches' Sabbath* shown at the London Coliseum in 1839.

The use of women and, increasingly, girls, to represent faeries on stage certainly helped to consolidate the abiding view of their appearance and temperament. This seems to be reflected in a popular music hall song, 'Oh, the fairies!'[21]

"Oh, the fairies; whoa the fairies,
Nothing but splendour and feminine gender.
Oh, the fairies; whoa the fairies,
Oh, for the wing of a fairy queen."

This verse forms the refrain of song about a drunken visit by two men to a Drury Lane pantomime and their anticipated ogling of the ballet girls performing there who- in truth- turn out to be "nothing like bright fairy land… all was so cold, no silver or gold/ The girls were amiss and misnamed." The ideal- from which the seedy reality fell so far short- was faeryland as a represented by a bevy of attractive girls in skimpy outfits. The "whoa" of the chorus conveys the blatant sexual dimension to this. Should there be any doubt on this point, Alfred Crowquill's humorous pamphlet *Pantomime As It Was and Will Be* (1849) illustrates stage faeries with an image of some bare legs being gradually revealed to the audience as the curtain rises at the start of a performance.

The same attitudes are seen in a verse by Arthur Symons, taken from his *London Nights* collection. He describes the dancers in a theatre:

"The little painted angels flit,
See, down the narrow staircase, where
The pink legs flicker over it!

Blonde and bewigged, and winged with gold,
The shining creatures of the air,
Troop sadly, shivering with cold."[22]

---

[21] Written and composed by T.S. Londsale & William G. Eaton, 1878; performed by George Leybourne (1842-1884).
[22] Symons, *Décor de Theatre,* '1. Behind the Scenes- Empire,' 1897.

Elsewhere Symons described one dancer, called Nora, as "Child, and most blithe, and wild as any elf.' For the Victorians, 'elf' had two meanings; one was anything petite and pretty; the second was a supernatural. But, by implication, that supernatural was a being of nature, untamed, unconstrained by human morals and (with luck) unencumbered by human garments. Nora, we should understand then, represented everything desirable: she was young, female, lithe and, we infer, of 'low' character and- as such- imbued with a 'natural' sexuality.[23]

For the Victorian male, therefore, the frisson of faeries on stage was all about those exposed legs and revealing tutus- and the assumption that a woman who was prepared to appear in public in such skimpy clothes was likely to have relaxed morals and therefore to be a good bet as an 'easy lay.' That sort of chauvinist thinking filtered through both from *and* to the faeries they pretended to be: they flitted around woods in minimal clothing and therefore, again, had to be sexually free (as Gilbert's lyrics hinted).

The highly gendered nature of fairies continued in the popular songs of the twenties and thirties of the next century, as with Beatrice Lilly (see later) and film star Gracie Fields' 1939 record 'The Fairy on the Christmas Tree.'

> "Every little girl would like to be
> The fairy on the Christmas tree-
> Up above the party dressed in white
> Shining in the candle-light!
>
> Every little boy has lots of fun,
> With his trumpet and his gun,
> Every little girl you understand,
> Is really Queen of Fairyland!

---

[23] Symons, 'Nora on the Pavement,' *Silhouettes,* 1896.

There's the little secret she must keep
That she can fly when she's asleep…"

Little girls (and, we understand, fairies) are perfect symbols of
femininity, dressed in white and raised up out of the way of
trouble (both physically on the tree and metaphorically within
society).  They have a sort of magic and dominion, but the
boys are the ones having fun with their pop-guns and trumpets
(innuendo surely intended).  This very sexist attitude to
women is also on display in the 1898 music hall song, 'My
Mary's a Fairy':

"My Mary's a fairy, light-hearted and airy.
Her eyes sparkle brightly, her laugh rings with glee;
She's spicy and witty, bewitchingly pretty,
And dresses as neatly as you'd wish to see."

By extension, 'fairy' could denote anything (but especially a
female) that was diminutive, dainty and delicate.  It was,
therefore, a term that was both a compliment of sorts and- at
the same time- condescending and demeaning.

The prospects could be bleak though, if a fairy didn't cast her
spell quickly enough, as Welsh music hall artiste Tessie
O'Shea admitted in 1934.[24]  Despite the jaunty, quirky tune,
this is the lament of an older woman whose silver star has lost
its glitter, whose tinsel is tarnished, whose wand is bent and
whose magic can no longer compete with that of younger girls.
She's overlooked by men now, because she has lost her
dimples and has moth holes in her tutu:

"For years a fairy queen I've been
For years I foiled the Demon King
But alas I'm getting on, the years have flown somehow
And I feel that Fairy Snowdrop isn't wanted now.

---

[24] *Nobody Loves a Fairy When She's Forty*, written by Arthur Le Clerq,
1934.

Nobody loves a fairy when she's forty,
Nobody loves a fairy when she's old."

The song exposes, but perpetuates, an assumption with which we still struggle- that all faeries are female, young and nubile. If they are old, they will be male.

"Whisper fairy stories 'til they're real"[25]

The appearance of faery in British rock music was the product of several converging trends.  The emergence of folk-rock created a genre within which it was possible to address more traditional, British themes that couldn't easily be accommodated within the parameters of American style rock and roll or blues.  Simultaneously, the development in the late 1960s of a counter-culture founded upon psychedelia helped to create a more welcoming environment for music based on fantasy and myth.  Tolkien's *Hobbit* and *Lord of the Rings* became popular reading and the first flickerings of an environmental movement gave impetus to a sense that westerners needed to reject consumerism, 'get back to the garden' and reconnect with the land.  Faeries, as nature spirits and as symbols of a native, non-industrialised culture, were highly attractive as subjects for songs as they indicated a band's sympathy with this sort of thinking.

Stirred into this mix was a revived taste for medievalising art- Pre-Raphaelite paintings, William Morris wallpapers and fabrics- and for Middle Age style clothes: flowing gowns for women and troubadour type outfits for men.  The Arthurian legends enjoyed renewed popularity- in part through the revival of Victorian literature (Tennyson and Morris) and the rediscovery of the work of Rossetti, Burne-Jones and others.  *Sir Gawain and the Greene Knight* was made into a film in 1973.

Musically, the time was right.  Late 1960s albums like *Sergeant Pepper's Lonely Hearts Club Band* had demonstrated the potential listenership for ambitious concept albums.  Rock music was developing into 'prog,' with an emphasis upon musicianship and 'serious' content.  Albums

---

[25] Vashti Bunyan, 'Glow Worms,' *Just Another Diamond Day,* 1970.

that dealt with literary or historical themes could now feasibly be recorded and released, musicians no longer felt themselves tied to the standard rock and roll preoccupations with love.

The music journalist Mike Barnes has written a history of progressive rock, *A New Day Yesterday.* His introduction is wryly entitled 'More Songs About Wizards and Hobbits,' reflecting the fact that many of his friends assumed, when they heard about his next writing project, that he would necessarily be spending his time discussing imaginary beings. Barnes wrote "The heyday of progressive rock is long enough ago now for received wisdom to suggest that it was all about wizards, elves and hobbits, and so it should be retrofitted thus and consigned to the dustbin of history. But, in fact, almost none of it had anything to do with this fantastical roll call." He also quoted a description of prog that he heard as "a twenty-minute flute solo followed by lyrics about hobbits." The emergence of progressive rock may have created the imaginative and creative atmosphere in which tracks about elves could be composed but, as Barnes recognised, it was scarcely restricted to this subject alone: "Lyrics encompassed social satire, invented worlds, sci-fi, ideas from literature, stream of consciousness word paintings, hippy-ish striving for enlightenment, a few love songs and even a smattering of politics."[26]

Prog was about far more than elves and hobbits, therefore, but under its liberal influence Faery, nevertheless, became entwined within the counterculture. *The Incredible String Band,* for example, included 'The Faeries Hornpipe' on their 1970 album 'U'. But then, NME journalist Neil Spencer described the band as a whole as the "apotheosis of mystical faerie-folke." A year earlier, *The Strawbs*, on their eponymous album, recorded 'Or Am I Dreaming,' in which they indulged every cliché of the genre:

---

[26] Barnes, *A New Day Yesterday,* 2020, 1-2 & 158.

"The fragile gentle butterfly with multi-coloured wings
Settles on the toadstools in the midst of fairy rings
Midsummer sounds of tinkle bells as sweet Titania
sings."

An intriguing contrast to such upbeat trivia is *The Kinks'*
bluesy 1966 track *Rainy Day in June:* doom and gloom
descend with the mist and rain and "the elves and gnomes
were hunched in fear/ Too terrified to cry."

Quintessential British prog rockers *Genesis* deployed themes
from folklore and myth in an even more subtle and surprising
manner. Their 1972 song 'Apocalypse in 9/8 (co-starring the
Delicious Talents of Gabble Ratchet)' makes mention in its
lyric of the English giant Magog and to the Pied Piper of faery
tale, whilst the title seems to be a clear reference to the
Gabriel Ratchets, the sky hounds or wild hunt of folklore. On
their album of the previous year, *Nursery Cryme,* the band
tackled the story of the *Fountain of Salmacis* (from Ovid's
*Metamorphoses*) which concerns the passion of a water
nymph for a beautiful boy.

The epitome- and nadir- of these influences is, probably, the
1984 live performance of *Stonehenge* by British rock band
*Spinal Tap,* in which dwarfish leprechauns in green dance
around a miniature trilithon to the sound of Celtic mandolin
and recorder. As this very well-known scene amply
demonstrates, the mystical, folk leanings of British rock can be
extremely easy targets to mock- they evoked a far-off land
where "children dance to the pipes of Pan… dewdrops cry and
the cats miaow," but their motivations were, nonetheless,
sincere and important.

## Pink Floyd

The first album released by Pink Floyd in August 1967 was
*Piper at the Gates of Dawn.* The title is taken from chapter
seven of Kenneth Grahame's *Wind in the Willows,* a strange,

slightly hallucinogenic episode in which Ratty and Mole meet the Great God Pan on an island, isolated at the end of a side branch of the river where they live. It's dawn and they are drawn inexorably into his presence, struck dumb with awe and reverence.[27]

As late as July in 1967, the intended title of the album had been *Projection*, but frontman Syd Barrett decided instead to borrow the name from one of his favourite books. Moreover, Barrett claimed to have had a dream, or vision, in which he met Pan (and other characters from the story) and the Great God had disclosed to him the secrets of the workings of Nature. Thereafter Barrett believed in tree spirits and, to some extent, even thought that this encounter had resulted in him being an earthly embodiment of the deity.

The album tracks themselves didn't refer to Pan, but there were still mythological references. The song *Matilda Mother* describes a child being read to in bed and the impact the fairy stories and their imagery have on his/ her imagination:

> "Wandering and dreaming
> The words have different meaning…
> For all the time spent in that room
> The doll's house, darkness, old perfume
> And fairy stories held me high on
> Clouds of sunlight floating by
> Oh mother, tell me more…"

Secondly, we have Barrett's song *The Gnome,* apparently drawing upon *Grimm's Fairy Tales* and the work of J. R. R. Tolkien, but full of traditional faery images and conventions. It concerns:

> "A gnome named Grimble Gromble
> And little gnomes stay in their homes

---

[27] See my discussion of this scene in *The Great God Pan,* Green Magic, 2021.

Eating, sleeping,
Drinking their wine.
He wore a scarlet tunic,
A blue green hood, it looked quite good
He had a big adventure
Amidst the grass, fresh air at last,
Wining, dining
Biding his time..."

As is well known, Barrett succumbed to drug use and was ejected from Pink Floyd before becoming a virtual recluse. Reading the lyrics, this may not entirely surprise us, but the songs begin to reveal the persistent and powerful influence of Pan and Faery in the British imagination, especially during the late 1960s and early '70s.

David Bowie

In April 1967 David Bowie released the single *Laughing Gnome*. In many respects this proved to be an episode he (and many of his fans) would rather have forgotten, but the record typified the antiquarian whimsy of many songs of the period, as already seen with Syd Barrett and as was also found in the work of Anthony Newley.

The single flopped at the time, but was re-released in 1973, after the advent of Ziggy Stardust, and sold well- despite the fact that the lyrics are a sickly combination of tradition, kitsch and absolutely terrible puns:

"I was walking down the high street
When I heard footsteps behind me
And there was a little old man
In scarlet and grey, shuffling away.
Well, he trotted back to my house
And he sat beside the telly
With his tiny hands on his tummy
Chuckling away, laughing all day

Oh, I ought to report you to the Gnome Office [Home Office] …

Ha ha ha, hee hee hee
I'm a laughing gnome and you don't catch me."

The visiting gnome is then entertained with "roasted toadstools and a glass of dandelion wine" before more excruciating 'jokes': for example, where does he come from? Gnome-man's land; plus metrognome, gnomads, the London School of Ecognomics, the BBC Gnome Service (Home Service). All of this is delivered in a squeaky little voice to a jaunty tune. The best that can be said is that it illustrates how certain preconceptions about the nature and appearance of gnomes had become embedded in British culture, despite the creatures having no place in authentic folk tradition.

A further curiosity single in the same vein is *Puckwudgie*, composed by May Holman and recorded by comedian Charlie Drake in 1972. The song takes its name from a supernatural being of the Ojibwa people, a spirit inherited by the white invaders from the native population through the works of the poets John Greenleaf Whittier and Henry Wadsworth Longfellow (*The Song of Hiawatha*). Both of these works transplanted the puckwudgie from the Great Lakes to New England and thereby introduced the being into popular culture and belief. Drake's UK single is a clear sign of that process. Threatening as these native spirits often were, the song itself is a highly whimsical ditty about this "little old bogeyman," who's transmuted into a leprechaun or brownie-type guardian:

"When I was young it made me jump when things went bump in the middle of the night
But as I got older I started getting bolder
Now I'm feeling really proud of myself...
But it's not so lonely when you know it's only a funny little fellow with a frown
Oh, Puckwudgie, will you see me through the night time for I feel better when you're there…

He's so small he lives in a wall at the bottom of the garden where the acorns fall
And, when the sun goes down, he starts on his rounds..."

With its cockney accent, rapid delivery and schoolchild chorus, the song is every bit as jaunty Bowie's, treating Faery in a light-hearted and irreverent manner. Despite his native American origins, puckwudgie is transplanted to a very southern English milieu, living at the bottom of the garden- along with Rose Fyleman's fairies.

This trend continued with another unfortunate novelty number, 'Do You Believe in Fairies?' by Rick Wakeman, included as a track on his 1982 album *Rock and Roll Prophet* and earlier released as the B-side of a single 'I'm So Straight I'm a Weirdo' in 1980. The track perpetuates the approach to Faery initiated by Bowie: sprightly bouncing music that indicates a fatal lack of seriousness (renouncing involvement even as you are engaged), squeaky voices and nonsense lyrics: "Pixies, elves, plastic gnomes/ Coming out of little homes..." The chorus asks "Do you believe in fairies/ Do you believe in love?" We may be driven to respond with a resounding 'no' to both enquiries.

To this same category of 'whimsical' faery rock, we should probably allocate 'Three Jolly Little Dwarves' by *Tomorrow*, released on their eponymous debut album in February 1968. The backing track is psychedelic, the best and most imaginative musical accompaniment of all the songs featured in this section. The lyrics, though, begin by perpetuating the fanciful view of folklore beings:

"Three jolly little dwarfs running round the meadow,
The sun is very, very bright leaving little shadows,
One wears red;
One wears green;
Another one blue;
Are they true?

Three jolly little dwarfs sitting on their toadstools,
They're such good company in their house so small..."

So far, so cute, like the other songs we've reviewed. However, a note of genuine fear enters the lyric: "the giant appears... his footsteps shake the ground/ And their little house falls down." In this tragic turn of events, the track takes on a tone authentic to much traditional folklore- and fairy tales, too, for that matter. It's a welcome exception to the attitude prevailing in the 'Laughing Gnome' and 'Puckwudgie,' which treat supernatural beings as (essentially) only fit for childish humour and- as such- merely harmless and humorous. This denigrates the real nature of faeries and it insults the listener, assuming that a junior audience can only cope with narratives that are cheerful and risk free.

Where, lastly, to mention *Gong's* 'Pot Head Pixies'? Between 1973-74 Virgin issued the band's *Radio Gnome* trilogy, which comprised the three albums *Flying Teapot, Angel's Egg* and *You*. Running through them all was the motif of Radio Gnome (apparently a means of telepathic communication) and the aforementioned pixies. They appear first on *Flying Teapot* and seem to be identical to the little green men mentioned in the song of the same name. The track 'Pot Head Pixies' (sort of) elaborates: they come from the sky in a flying teapot having travelled from the green Planet Gong, the planet of love. "I am, you are, we are, crazy!" they declare in a stoned voice- they sing a catchy song and they want people to "be aware... they just can't give you enough." Gong's tunes can certainly be catchy, but they're also spaced out and weird, with fractured rhythms and strange instrumentation- in a way that's very welcome after what's gone before.

The track 'Zero the Hero and the Witch's Spell' makes clear the power that these supernaturals exert:

"I love you mister Pixie...
All I want to do is to be you.

I love your face
I love your space
I love your rays, baby
And if you like, I'll stay tonight."

This is *Ziggy Stardust*, but stoned. We meet the pixies again on *Angel's Egg*- flying around inner space in their teapot taxis and sending "kisses in the brain," after which the listener is advised:

"You know just who,
the pot head pixies are-
Have a little drink."[28]

Finally, on *You,* the song 'A PHP's Advice' is dispensed:

"Let a pothead pixie
tell you what to do
And this is what he'll tell you:
If you've got a problem
to know who you are,
Hear now this is what you do-
Remember
You are me; I am you
all of us together- now go
AUM."

Having a little drink may be the last thing the listener needs, but we can be reasonably sure that the pixies offer an interplanetary message of Eastern mysticism, peace and love, all enjoyed with a spliff and a pot of mushroom tea. These are pixies, but not as we know them...

Whilst on the subject of Gong and uncategorisable songs, we might as well include here 'Sea Nature' by Steve Hillage, a former Gong guitarist. The lead track on his 1978 album,

---

[28] *Angel's Egg,* 'Oily Way,' 'Love is How You Make It' and 'I Never Glid Before.'

*Green,* this song is the only one that- to my knowledge- discusses devas and the Findhorn community of Moray in Scotland. Devas are Indian supernatural or celestial beings that were imported into western culture as nature spirits by the Theosophists. They were ranked alongside faeries and brownies by such figures as Geoffrey Hodson in his book *Fairies at Work and Play* (1925).

Over a jazzy, funky tune and bluesy guitar soloing, Hillage invites us:

> "I want you to come with me,
> Journeying with your mind;
> We'll learn to feel the Devas
> And feed them with our vibes
> Hear the music of the spheres through the ears of the cauliflowers,
> And the living grass that breathes."

Hillage's devas of course have nothing to do with British faery tradition- but neither do the North American puckwudgie or gnomes- which were invented in the sixteenth century by German physician Paracelsus. British faerylore has always been something of a hybrid, deriving vitality from external influences. A substantial part of this book will be concerned with the impact of J. R. R. Tolkien's elves and dwarves, which were themselves a compound of literary and traditional influences. The significant thing, I think, is the yearning for the supernatural that is demonstrated by all this music. People still find personal and musical inspiration in myth and legend.

Marc Bolan- *A Gift from the Fair Folk*

> "And then he sang,
> notes true and full,
> pure as the pearly horn of unicorn,
> lithe as a fairy dance."[29]

---

[29] from the *Warlock of Love*, 1967.

Much of the British rock music of the late sixties and early seventies was suffused with Faery, but one of the best examples of this is the work of Marc Bolan, in the days when he performed as *Tyrannosaurus Rex*, and before he shortened the band name to *T. Rex* and became the glam star for which he is best remembered.

The fairy influence is especially strong in the four albums Bolan released between 1968 and 1970, but even as late as *Ride a White Swan* in 1972 there are traces of elvishness. The album titles themselves betray the tenor of the songs included on them: they are *My People Were Fair and Had Sky in Their Hair… But Now they're Content to Wear Stars on Their Brows* (which is all one title and was taken from a saying by Tom Bombadil in Tolkien's *Lord of the Rings*) and *Prophets, Seers and Sages,* both issued during 1968; 1969's *Unicorn* and, lastly, *A Beard of Stars,* released in the following year.

A Crooning Moon Rune

"Legends we long for and legends there are…"[30]

Musically, Bolan was deeply inspired by *Pink Floyd*'s Syd Barrett. Barrett was, he declared, "One of the few people I'd actually call a genius. He inspired me beyond belief."

Following Barrett's lead, certain themes appear repeatedly on Bolan's late sixties albums. There are, of course, repeated allusions to dwarves and fairies:

"Twelve years old, your elvish fingers toss your Beethoven hair"[31]

"You're a gift from the fair folk…

---

[30] Marc Bolan, *The Warlock of Love.*
[31] 'Child Star,' on *My People.*

A sprite in my house of sight."[32]

"Fairy lights in her eyes
Tame the water."[33]

"She bathes in thunder
The elves are under her."[34]

"Tree wizard pure tongue …
The swan king, the elf lord."[35]

"Fools have said the hills are dead
But her nose is a rose of the Shee;
A silver sword by an ancient ford,
Was my gift from the child of the trees."[36]

There are, too, plentiful mentions of wizards, warlocks and
magi, of myths and legends and of mysterious creatures, such
as unicorns.  Bolan references C. S. Lewis' *Narnia* ('Wonderful
Brown-Skin Man' on *Prophets*); King Arthur and the Matter of
Britain: "Holy Grail Head, deep forest fed/ Weaving deep
beneath the moon" ('Conesuala' on *Prophets*) or "Let's make a
quest for Avalon" *('Stones for Avalon,'* on *Unicorn*), and
(repeatedly) Beltane, including these lines:

> "Wear a tall hat like a druid in the old days,
> Wear a tall hat and a tattooed gown,
> Ride a white swan like the people of the Beltane…"[37]

Beltane wasn't just a pagan festival for Bolan, it was also a
fantasy land that he'd invented, in imitation of Narnia and

---

[32] 'Travelling tragition,' on *Prophets*.
[33] 'Pilgrim's Tale,' on *Unicorn*.
[34] 'Jewel,' *T. Rex*, 1970.
[35] 'Suneye,' *T. Rex*.
[36] 'Blessed Wild Apple Girl,' *Best of T.Rex*, 1971.  The *shee* are the faeries
of Scotland (*sith*) and Ireland (*sidhe*).  In this case, Bolan's mention of a
rose makes me suspect that these lines were inspired by W. B. Yeats.
[37] 'Ride a White Swan,' on *Ride a White Swan*, 1972

Middle Earth. It was the setting for a novel, *The Krakenmist,* which he wrote in 1968; he had intended it also to be the basis of an entire concept album, which for better or worse was never written. In his 1969 collection of poems, *Warlock of Love,* we encounter very similar concepts: a "winter witch," the "fluted floors of Dagamoor" and the "wars of Faragadan." There seem, too, to be woodland nymphs or dryads, as in the lines:

> "Daughters of love unite
> Encircle our woody globe
> And blow at the smouldering hearts of youth."

Certainly, Bolan could see spirits in the natural elements: rain was "the nymphet of Nature's nourishment" in one of the *Warlock of Love* verses. What the poetry from that collection demonstrates, I think, is that Bolan was not much of a poet; the imagery is disjointed, if not incoherent. In a work of literary pretensions, this can be problematic; in song lyrics, where sound and effect are more important, it is far less of a drawback.

Bolan was, it seems, steeped in British folklore. He wrote of 'The Misty Coast of Albany' (with its echoes of Blake's rocky shores of Albion) and of the magical woods "Elder, elm and oak." ('Iscariot' and 'Misty Coast,' both on *Unicorn*). Even so, the other major fascination and inspiration for him seems to have been classical myth, most especially woodland creatures like satyrs and fauns. On a mantelpiece at his home, he kept a small green statute of the god Pan, which he called 'Poon' and to whom he addressed little messages and requests. Bolan's biographer Mark Paytress has described the god as "Marc's muse." Of course, in this devotion he's linked directly to Arnold Bax, John Ireland, Granville Bantock and Arthur Machen and so sits within a lineage of British writing.[38] Poon appeared on the cover of *A Beard of Stars* and was mentioned in songs- directly in the hypnotic chant 'Puckish Pan,' an

---

[38] See my *Great God Pan,* 2021.

unfinished track which was never released, and allusively in the spirit of the song 'Woodland Bop.'

The pagan Greek world appears explicitly several times in Bolan's lyrics, with allusions to satyrs, maenads and titans:

"The frowning moon, it tans the faun,
Who holds the grapes for my love."[39]

"a pagan temple to Zeus,
He drinks acorn juice"[40]

"Alice eyes scan the mythical scene…
We ran just like young fauns…"[41]

As this jumble of citations further confirms, there were so many allusions packed into Bolan's songs that the verses tended not to tell any sequential story but rather to sketch impressionistic imagery for the listener: aural painting, let's say, creating a mood or feeling.

The jumble of influences and imagery extended to the band's album covers, too. Bolan loved the art of William Blake, Dali and Arthur Rackham and for the cover of the first album, *My People,* asked the designer to provide something that looked 'like Blake.' On the back of the sleeve of *Unicorn* there's a black and white photo of Bolan and co-member Steve Peregrine Took (note the name, Tolkien fans). The pair are posed with an array of meaningful objects, which include a book on the Cottingley fairies (supplied by photographer Peter Sanders) and several volumes from Bolan's own collection- a child's Shakespeare, Khalil Gibran's *The Prophet* and William Blake's collected verse. Collectively, these form a kind of key to Bolan's writing.

---

[39] 'Frowning Atahualpa,' *My People.*
[40] 'Stacey Grove,' *Prophets.*
[41] 'Scenescof Dynasty,' *Prophets.*

"And with the coming of the sweet breath,
the seeds in the garden of all hearts
will flower immense,
and such flames licking and long,
will be sighted upon our lands,
that it will seem to the highborn
that the Earth has hatched anew."[42]

Bolan knew the power of the right literary references and that his audiences would identify with them, even if only at a subliminal level. On June 9th 1972, the *Melody Maker* published a review of a Bolan gig at the Birmingham Odeon. A good deal of this piece was given over to taking the fans' reactions. Noelle, aged fifteen and from Kilsby in Northamptonshire, had travelled to Brum for the show and explained how Marc was "a brilliant poet... He believes in the little people and reminds you of a different world." Bolan himself told the magazine *Gandalf's Garden* that "the texture of the past interests me." He never wrote for the future, he claimed, instead borrowing names and strings of words as the basis from which to gain his inspiration and from which to create his songs. Indeed, in the poetry collection, *The Warlock of Love,* he described himself "uttering words of poetry in magical wordways." Bolan also declared a deep love of the countryside- to the extent that *My People Were Fair* was a collection of "woodland songs" which he had written whilst in the country.

Bolan liked to build up his supernatural mystique, even claiming that he had spent time in France training as a wizard. He told the *London Evening Standard* that this had included studying both black and white magic and that he had considered performing a "rite of Pan" which would have transformed him into a satyr- but he had chickened out because he had become scared about what would happen then- would he be hunted or put in a zoo; would he ever be able turn himself back into a human again? Perhaps he would

---

[42] from *Warlock of Love.*

have become the being he described in his volume of poetry, *The Warlock of Love*:

> "Motion toed,
> loping up the hillocks of youth
> like a furry soul,
> drinking with your sweet springing mouth,
> hooded by the stream of Pan."

## Do You Ken John Peel?

The Bolan story is made more intriguing for his association with radio DJ John Peel.  Peel will be well known to many British readers, but very possibly less familiar to those from outside the UK.  He became an institution on BBC Radio One, with a weekly show late on Friday nights on which he played and promoted new music he had discovered.  He played a major role introducing listeners to punk rock from 1976, but before that had favoured folk and dub.  Earlier still, he had been a good friend of Marc Bolan.

The pair met in late July or early August 1967 and quickly became close.  They spent a great deal of time together, professionally and socially, and Bolan one night gave Peel a hamster called Biscuit (in a night club- the poor creature spent the evening riding round on one of the turntables).

Peel was taken with Bolan's warbling voice and began to feature *Tyrannosaurus Rex* prominently on his radio shows. He wrote a regular column in the *International Times* in which he also promoted his new friend.  As an established and respected DJ Peel played frequently around the country and so could offer more direct help to his friend's career.  He started to give Bolan live support sets to his DJ appearances: Peel had a regular slot at the club called *Middle Earth* in London's Covent Garden and also took the band with him as part of his 'John Peel Roadshow' as it was grandly called- in

73

reality, everyone crammed together in his car and heading up the motorway.

Not only did Peel promote Bolan's music; he contributed to it. He narrated the track *Wood Story* on the album *My People Were Fair* and wrote the sleeve notes:

> "They rose out of the sad and scattered leaves of an older summer… They blossomed with the coming spring, children rejoiced and the earth sang with them. It will be a long and ecstatic summer."

Peel provided a further narration on the album *Unicorn* and also started to appear as a sort of support act for his friend. He read poetry to the crowd at the Royal Albert Hall, sitting cross-legged on the stage, and at the *Tyrannosaurus Rex* gig at the Queen Elizabeth Hall on January 13th 1969, Peel was billed to appear to "prove the existence of fairies," as the flyers promised, by reading poetry to the audience. In the face of this proof, they remained, it is reported, "politely silent." What could Peel have been reading? Based on what we learned just now, I wonder if the DJ may have read selected poems from Shakespeare and Blake- and maybe John Keats too?

Peel made out later that he never really understood or sympathised with Bolan's mythic leanings. He claimed that he couldn't understand the song lyrics because they were too 'mystical' and 'hippie' for him. Nonetheless, there's the evidence of those sleeve notes and we know too that the pair travelled, with their respective partners, to visit Glastonbury, capital of hippiedom since the days of Rutland Boughton, where Bolan was pictured on top of the Tor.

In later years Peel was a gruff and slightly cynical personality, so these 'airy-fairy' indulgences all feel rather difficult to reconcile with the older, more rational enthusiast for the *Sex Pistols* and *Extreme Noise Terror*. Nevertheless, Peel's overall verdict was that *Tyrannosaurus Rex* "were elfin to a degree beyond human understanding."

74

Marc Bolan is now the best remembered fairy rock star of the period, but the fae influence was all-pervasive at the time. The 'airy-fairy' attitudes Bolan brought to dealing with the supernatural were- as we've already seen- very far from being uniquely his own. He inherited them- doubtless unquestioningly- from childhood story books and from popular songs; from fine art and from literature. These unconscious influences he shared with many other artists. Later we'll discuss the contemporary work of the folk singer Donovan Leitch. For now, a song by *Manfred Mann's Earth Band* will serve to underline the point. Their track, 'Spirits in the Night,' which features on the 1975 album *Nightingales and Brothers,* ostensibly concerns beings termed 'gypsy angels' who are:

> "built like light and they dance like
> Spirits in the night, all night
> Oh, you don't know what they can do to you…
> Stand right up and let them shoot through you."

In this ability to pass through solid barriers- and in their habit of enjoying themselves on bright moonlit nights- these creatures bear a very strong resemblance to the commonest class of fairies. What's more, they dance to a "soul fairy band." The narrator of the song then has sex with 'Janey,' who:

> "… kissed me just right
> Like only a lonely angel can
> She felt so nice, just as soft as a
> Spirit in the night…"

The insubstantiality, combined with intense sensuality, epitomises one vision of the faery female. All the same, different reading could lead to very different perceptions of faery females, as we shall now see.

Whilst not avowedly a 'faery' song, it is very hard to discuss the fae spirit in seventies rock without making mention of *Stairway to Heaven*, released in 1971. The song starts as an archetypal example of folk rock, with acoustic guitar and recorders, and the lyrics might also be seen as an attempt to score Tolkien's *Lord of the Rings*.

In a later chapter, we'll consider what 'fairy music' might be like, but the famous introduction to *Stairway to Heaven* must sound entirely suitable to many people. The recorders and acoustic guitar- peaceful, beautiful and distinctly wistful- achieve the perfect tone. The tune has resemblances a traditional folk song, which may seem surprising, but Robert Plant and Jimmy Page both acknowledge the inspiration they have drawn from English folk singer Anne Briggs.

Over and above the clear influence of the Middle Earth stories, I think it is possible to construct a reasonable argument to the effect that *Stairway to Heaven* is firmly founded upon authentic British fairy tradition.

> "There's a lady who's sure all that glitters is gold
> And she's buying a stairway to heaven…"

It is a regular feature of the folklore that fairy gold is not to be trusted. When used in payment to a human, it will almost always turn out to be dried leaves, pebbles, shells, mushrooms or even pellets of horse dung; in other words, worthless and a sign of faery duplicity. In the song, though, the money offered by this mysterious lady is exactly what it seems to be- perhaps because she's in earnest or because she's dealing with her own kind. This last possibility seems likeliest when she is mentioned again later as a lady "we all know." This inclusiveness also serves to draw the listener further into the song, one of the subtle reasons for its abiding success.

"There's a feeling I get when I look to the west
And my spirit is crying for leaving."

There is a strong echo of Tolkien here, when the elves depart for the west at the end of *Lord of the Rings,* but there are resonances with faerylore too. In Wales the *tylwyth teg,* also called the *Plant Rhys Dwfn,* are to be found living on islands off the west coast of the nation, places men long to visit but which are only rarely visible or accessible. Just like these *Green Islands of the Flood,* in Ireland the 'Land of Youth,' *Tír na nÓg,* is also to be found out in the Atlantic to the west. These lines therefore tap-in to a cultural yearning for a better, mystical land, nearby but out of ordinary mortal reach.

"And it's whispered that soon, if we all call the tune
Then the piper will lead us to reason
And a new day will dawn for those who stand long
And the forests will echo with laughter…"

Across Britain, fairykind are known for their music, song and dancing. Frequently, however, their dances within faery rings are used as a means of entrapment against unwary humans. Here, though, it appears that a more benign experience is envisaged (just as with the lady's gold) and that participation in the dance will have a positive outcome. An effort is required: the individual must "you listen very hard" but it will be rewarded. Only joy and resolution will come from our contact; there will be laughter and wealth, though not necessarily material gain, as the lady's gold may not be mere currency but some spiritual renewal. That this is the case is suggested by the reassurance that her quest may be achieved even if the "stars [stores] are all closed."

"In a tree by the brook, there's a songbird who sings…
In my thoughts I have seen rings of smoke through the trees
And the voices of those who stand looking…"

Altogether, there's something deeply British about this nostalgia for an unspoilt rural environment: smoke rising from cottage chimneys, birds singing in woodland, a more innocent and contented time. Robert Plant continues by telling us that "there are two paths you can go by," a line that conjures up the different routes shown to Thomas of Erceldoune by the Faery Queen (to heaven, hell and Faery). The listener's head is humming, perhaps from scrumpy, but definitely with the subtle references to fairy tales and proverbial sayings (the piper- of Hamelin; the rock that doesn't roll- which incorporates, too, a nod of awareness to the fact that this is a rock song). These deft allusions all help to situate the song within comforting tradition- and childhood.

The present is presented as something to be escaped; the modern world is polluted and corrupted by industry, pollution and greed- and those dark satanic mills of William Blake lurk, unspoken but consciously acknowledged, in the background of the song. *Stairway to Heaven* is a song of yearning- a longing to make a change and to return to a Britain of yesteryear, to a simpler, better age of communal unity: "When all is one and one is all." The individual will be able to join with "those who stand looking" and, together, achieve the "new dawn."

"Sometimes all of our thoughts are misgiven…"

What will be escaped, as well, is the duplicity and falseness of the modern world. We are warned that sometimes "words have two meanings" and that all of our thoughts may be "misgiven"- the rather archaic word only helping to reinforce the medieval tone of the song, rather as if it were a traditional ballad.

The lady, however, stands for certainty. Her word has magical power and she is assured that she can achieve her purpose. We can rely upon her and she will show us "how everything still turns to gold;" through some almost alchemical transformation a better society can be established. Once again, it seems that Robert Plant is consciously using themes from British faery tradition to new ends: many folk tales examine the faeries' commitment to the literal meaning of words and bargains, and the personal duty to keep your promises.

As for that "lady we all know," she trails behind her connotations of the Virgin Mary as well as of the Faery Queen. In addition, she is explicitly some form of nature spirit, a green woman even:

> "If there's a bustle in your hedgerow, don't be alarmed now
> It's just a spring clean for the May Queen..."

The faeries are a rural people, living in close harmony with the plants and creatures of the countryside. Part of their function seems to be the maintenance of the balance of nature- but also they may work for spiritual renewal.[43] Accordingly, the 'Lady' in the song is a female counterpart of the Green Man; she's the White Goddess of the hawthorn discussed by Robert Graves in his influential book of 1961.[44] She "shines white light"- evidence of her magical power- and is at one with the elements, such as the "whispering wind." She is the spirit of nature invoked by well-dressing and other traditional ceremonies; she is Galadriel sailing away from Middle Earth; she is one of those Arthurian maidens- Morgan le Fay perhaps.

For British audiences- at least- *Stairway to Heaven* resonated with layer after layer of meaning and memory. It reminded us that Faery and enchantment were still to be found, despite industrialisation and urbanisation, engrained in the fabric of the British Isles, pregnant within sites in the landscape. This song highlighted the light and hope in the British tradition; but there was a darker and more despairing side to it, too.[45]

---

[43] See my *Faeries and the Natural World,* 2021, for more on this subject.
[44] *The White Goddess*, Faber and Faber, 1961.

Less well known is the Led Zeppelin song, *The Battle of Evermore,* which comprises an even more direct embodiment of Tolkien's heroic mythology in song. In quick succession, we are introduced to the Queen of Light, the Prince of Peace, the Dark Lord, dragons, ring-wraiths and the Angels of Avalon. There are the same pastoral references, to "The apples of the valley [which] hold/ The seeds of happiness" but the mood is sombre, for this bucolic refuge lies under a threat of war- just as does Middle Earth. The rural calm is shattered and the tone is one of endurance- hanging on through the depths of night until the "eastern glow" returns. In *Stairway to Heaven* there is a longing for twilight and stars coming out; in *The Battle of Evermore,* a sense of balance can only be restored in daylight through magic runes and mortal struggle. The refrain is "bring it back," but what's to be restored is not a golden age so much as a shattered routine of daily farming chores. Further Tolkien references appear in the song *Misty Mountain Hop* (I'm packing my bags for the Misty Mountains/ Where the spirits go now) and *Ramble On* (mentions of Gollum and "darkest depths of Mordor").

Music journalist Mike Barnes has joked that *Led Zeppelin*'s oeuvre can be criticised as being entirely about shagging, except for a few songs about hobbits- and even some of those are about shagging hobbits. Barnes rejected this misrepresentation of the band's output, which debases and devalues its content and, as I hope this section has shown, their treatment of supernatural themes could, in fact, be both subtle and complex.[46]

The faery queen as a figure of awe and power, rather than a graceful and pretty sprite, was a traditional image that regained its potency from the late 1960s onwards, thereby restoring to her much of the majesty that she had lost as she

---

[45] See once again my *Faeries and the Natural World,* 2021, for more on the faeries as spirits of place.
[46] Barnes, *New Day Yesterday,* 158-159.

dwindled to mere wish-granting fairy godmother. The American band *Blue Öyster Cult* imagined a 'Celestial Queen' somewhere between these two poles. The singer finds himself out of his own world, where "There's no place for one of my kind." The celestial queen seems to be some kind of dominatrix mistress- her fairy laughter is heard, but it's the sound of scorn and abandonment:

> "She came from the dark, she came from a dream,
> All leather and chain the rising queen
> Born into the night, born into the spotlight,
> She spread her wings and then she was gone."[47]

The supernatural monarch truly is a 'killer queen.' Perhaps the song also explains the experience of Ozzy Osbourne, who going home late at night (whether or not from the pub is not made clear), has a fright when he sees inside a house:

> "Fairy boots are dancing with a dwarf...
> Yeah, fairies wear boots, and you've got to believe me-
> Yeah, I saw it... I tell you no lies."[48]

His doctor blames the vision on too much dope; it certainly probably helped.

## Queen: "A Fairy Fellow"

If we are discussing progressive rock- a music with clear literary and artistic pretensions- we can hardly ignore the early albums of *Queen*. Rather like Marc Bolan, there was some attempt to construct a fantasy realm in these- *The Seven Seas of Rhye* on the album, *Queen I* of 1973- as well as a clear commitment to mythical themes, something that was clearest from the *Queen II* album of 1974.

---

[47] From the album *Spectres,* 1977.
[48] *Black Sabbath,* from *Paranoid,*

This second album is divided into white and black sides, the latter comprising what Freddie Mercury termed "little fairy stories." Faery is very apparent in tracks such as 'White Queen' (white side) and, on the black side, 'Ogre Battle' and 'The March of the Black Queen.' We have archaic diction "How did thee fare, what have thee seen/ The mother of the willow green," conscious fairy tale constructions ("once upon a time, an old man told me a fable"), as well as allusions to the Goddess, pipers and black crows. *The White Queen (As it Begab)* is a lovely tune and could easily be a medieval trouvere's song of courtly love: "It's for evermore that I wait." The idolised woman, who's termed "goddess" as well as queen, could very easily be the same 'Lady' as in *Stairway to Heaven*: she has "stars of lovingness in her hair" and is wrapped in mystery as she walks at night.

However, two tracks make Queen's fae influence very clear. On the first album there is the song *My Fairy King*. It is set in a land where horses are born with eagle wings and the honey bees have lost their stings, an Edenic place where the rivers flow with wine, there is perpetual singing, and lions lie down with deer. The land is controlled by an omnipotent and omniscient monarch:

> "My fairy king can see things…
> That are not there for you and me…
> My fairy king can do right and nothing wrong."

However, evil men threaten to destroy this paradise:

> "… someone has drained the colour from my wings,
> Broken my fairy circle ring,
> And shamed the king in all his pride…"

Freddie Mercury's vision of Faery is, in fact, much more like a heaven threatened by Satan than any fairyland of folk tradition.

The band's second album, *Queen II,* features on its 'black' side the track *The Fairy Feller's Master Stroke,* which is nothing more or less than a word-picture description of the painting of that title by Victorian artist Richard Dadd, now in the Tate Gallery in London. It's reported that Mercury repeatedly visited the Tate to study the picture and insisted that his fellow band members did the same. The album was released in March 1974, which means that it must predate the Tate's touring exhibition of 1974-75, *The Late Richard Dadd, 1817-1886,* but Mercury's intense fascination with the picture surely suggests that he would have attended the show and further deepened his knowledge of the painting.

Richard Dadd wrote a very long poem to explain the imagery of his work (the full text is given in Coda One). Dated 'January 1865, Broadmoor secure hospital,' it is titled *Elimination of a picture and its subject- called the Feller's Master Stroke*.[49] It appears that Mercury was very well acquainted with this verse and that he borrowed numerous elements from it for his own lyrics.

Despite his own serious mental health problems, the verse indicates that Dadd realised that his crowded picture needed some sort of guide or key:

> "To where a canvas glowed
> With fays, a leafy node
> Encircling wild about."

The poem is convoluted and rambling, entirely lacking the "sense as terse/ As poets jam into a measured line" that Dadd apparently sought. The painting originated in "pure fancy," he states, based not any fairy story or folk tradition (although there are many authentic elements present- such as a faery dairy maid and Queen Mab herself). Rather, the scene is fantastical, created "as in a trance" for "common nature is not true." Dadd then proceeds to describe all the characters he

---

[49] See the appendix for the full text of this verse.

painted, who comprise the spectrum of faery society. He identifies amongst them a satyr and a dandy with a nymph- all of them very "queer."

Even where he's not quoting directly, Mercury paraphrases and condenses Dadd's words:

> "He's a fairy feller
> The fairy folk have gathered 'round the new moon shine
> To see the feller crack a nut at night's noon time…"

Dadd's picture is a dense image of multiple faery figures of different sizes and wildly varied dress, from Oberon and Titania down to the humblest of the faery realm. Mercury in turn examines all of these with rapt attention, the rapid and layered lyrics reflecting the crammed nature of the canvas itself:

> "a satyr peers under lady's gown, dirty fellow
> What a dirty laddio…
> Fairy dandy tickling the fancy of his lady friend;
> The nymph in yellow…
> What a quaere fellow…"

Rock journalist Simon Reynolds has made a convincing case to the effect that *Fairy Feller* may be read as a declaration of gay identity by Freddie Mercury. It doesn't seem unreasonable to suppose that the 'fairy feller' and the 'queer fellow' of the lyrics refer to the vocalist himself, discretely expressing his sexuality under cover of artistic code. Nonetheless, much of the lyric derives from Dadd (chosen, I presume, because it did seem so congenial to Mercury) and I think that the song can still be regarded in itself as one of the greatest expressions of Faery in modern rock.[50]

With its choral backing vocals, exaggerated operatic enunciation and harpsichord like accompaniment, the track is

---

[50] Reynolds, *Shock and Awe- Glam Rock & Its Legacy*, 2016, 461-2.

very clearly written by the group that would compose 'Bohemian Rhapsody' in a couple of years' time.  As an attempt to set a Victorian faery painting to music, it is, needless to say, utterly unique.

## Tom Newman

Newman was the producer of Mike Oldfield's epochal album, *Tubular Bells,* the first issue of the new label *Virgin Records* and Oldfield's first release since the *Sallyangie*'s ill-fated 1968 recording.  The young Oldfield, who was still in his teens, played almost all the instruments on the album, with Newman combining numerous tracks to create the final product.  Part of the appeal of the record was Oldfield's guitar playing, but he was assisted in this by a new effects-pedal he had acquired, a bit of kit called the 'Glorfindel Box.'  Glorfindel is an elf of Middle Earth, mentioned several times in *Lord of the Rings.*

After the huge success of *Tubular Bells,* Newman went on to produce Oldfield's other mid-seventies albums, *Ommadawn* and *Hergest Ridge.*  The latter release showed a taste for folk and world music that his sister Sally was later to explore further, as we shall see.  Newman, meanwhile, issued his own instrumental album much in the vein of Oldfield's releases.  *The Faerie Symphony* of 1977 is an electric, folk-tinged epic comprising thirteen tracks.  These tunes don't flow into each other, as did Oldfield's, which enables them to be named individually.  They include *Bean Si* (a more authentic spelling of banshee), *The Little Voices of the Tarans,*[51] *The Seelie* (and *Unseelie*) *Courts,*[52] *The Dance of the Daoine Sidhe* (another Gaelic term, meaning the faery folk) and a cover of Rutland Boughton's *The Fairy Song,* from the *Immortal Hour,* making very clear the tracks' subject and inspiration.  The tunes have a 'Celtic' style and feature an ensemble of bagpipes, flageolets, balalaika, glockenspiel, gongs and electric guitar, creating a sound very similar to that of *Tubular*

---

[51] A type of Gaelic supernatural, the spirits of unbaptised babies.
[52] The good and bad faeries of Scottish folk tradition.

*Bells.* These comparisons are not meant to detract from or diminish the album, which can be charming and highly listenable, including some beautiful tunes and anthems, albeit alongside some more challenging feedback and jazzy freak out moments...

In May 2021, Newman released *Faery Symphony II.* The tracks include the suitably titled *Theena Shee* (a phonetic spelling of the earlier *Daoine Sidhe), Faerie Waltz* and *The Lordly Ones* (a reference to Fiona Macleod). Newman is quoted as saying that the new album "is not intended to be comfortable, predictable or commercial."

## Folk, Rock and Steeleye Span

The new genre of folk-rock that emerged in the later sixties inevitably incorporated faery themes, whether these were derived from the traditional songs and ballads that the artists covered or were elements in their own compositions. Scottish singer Donovan Leitch is a good exemplar of this. His second album, released in 1965, was titled *Fairy Tale,* whilst a single from that year, 'Turquoise,' described riding a faery stallion through the sky. The singer's 1971 double album, *HMS Donovan,* is replete with faery allusions. The penultimate track is the song 'Queen Mab'- a track he re-released on a 2017 compilation called *Living Crystal Faery Realm.* Leitch's 'Mab' is not the robust monarch of seventeenth century tradition, but the kind of fluttery fairy popularised by children's stories over the last century and a half. She is a little fairy who comes at night:

> "her eyes are blue and her hair is brown
> With silver spots upon her wings
> And from the moon she flutters down."

This saccharine fae bears a little silver wand, too, another Victorian/ Disney innovation, but- more faithful to Queen Mab's reputation as a midwife of dreams (as portrayed in

*Romeo and Juliet*)- she visits good children in bed and conjures up "dreams of pleasant things," fairy tale scenes of wonderous gardens and "pretty dwarfs to show the way/ Through fairy hills and fairy dales."[53]

The same 1971 album depicts several other rather twee and harmless fairies. The song, 'Things to Wear,' takes the form of a catalogue of magical items of apparel, in a curious jumble of authentic lore and whimsy. If you wear a ring woven from grass, "you can hear the fairies sing/ As they pass;" a daisy chain will let you hear the goblin train whistling as it "dives beneath a thistle" and tying your shoe with blades of grass will help you to dream of faery glades. 'Can Ye Dance' is a ditty about a fairy reel, played for an elf in silver sandals, whilst the 'Seller of Stars' in the song of that name weaves wings for the fairies. Depending upon your view of fairykind, therefore, 'Little Ben' may come as a sombre contrast, for it seems to be about a boy abducted by the Rowan Fairy, Gwindle, a spirit of the mountain ash. Given her rather twee name, I very much suspect that Donovan sees this taking in a romantic and positive light, which is rather counter to the tragedy inherent in most folklore accounts of such cases.

In his 2021 song *I Am the Shaman,* Donovan continued to sing about dainty faery themes:

> "Yon wheeling of great stars
> Hath cast a silver web around my heart
> Upon an Elfin-Sea
> In a ship of filigree…"

It wasn't just *Led Zeppelin* who were acutely sensitive to the Britishness of Faery, therefore. Several other folk-rock bands tackled traditional faery themes in a serious way. *Jethro Tull* did so in 'Mayhem, Maybe' an Irish tinged jig which describes how a village is assailed at night, its inhabitants tormented for

---

[53] For more about Mab, see my *Famous Faeries,* 2020.

the amusement of the faeries: scattering horses, shredding hedges and scaring people and animals:

> "As us fairy folks sweep from the hill
> Never caught us and never will.
> Pulling roses and daffodils-
> Mayhem in the high degree."[54]

*Steeleye Span* were also active in the same field. Bob Johnson of the band explained his attachment to his native land and its mythology- and how this fed into his own creativity- in an interview in 1976:

> "Everything I do and think is based on England. If I lived on the West Coast [of the USA] how on earth could I think about elves and fairies and goblins and old English castles and churches?"

That said, the band recorded a version of a traditional Danish ballad, 'Eline af Villenskov,' for their 1974 album, *Now We Are Six*. The original is a song about trolls, but its English title is 'Seven Hundred Elves.' The elves object to a man who tries to settle and cultivate in their wood. The poor farmer is only just able to save himself with the sign of the cross on all his goods when:

> "Seven hundred elves from out the wood
> Foul and grim they were
> Down to the farmer's house they went
> His meat and drink to share."

The song that formed the basis of 'Seven Hundred Elves' came from the Danish folk collection *Danmarks gamle Folkeviser* (Old Danish Folk Songs) a volume which also contained the ballad 'Sir Olof.' This was adapted as *Dance with Me* for *Span*'s 1975 album *All Around My Hat*. This track is an account of a knight riding through the greenwood who is

---

[54] From *The Broadsword & the Beast,* 1982.

invited to dance with the elf king's daughter, in return for which she promises him golden spurs and a fine white shirt. The scenario seems innocent and unthreatening enough, but a knowledge of the dangers inherent in entering dances in faery rings suggests the profound peril the knight faces by consenting. In 1996 the band also recorded a version of the traditional Scots ballad 'Lady Isabel and the Elf Knight' and they have played 'Tam Lin' live numerous times.

Far more significant for this book, though, was an independent project by two members of *Span*. So strong, in fact, was the influence of the spirit of place that Johnson had referred to that, along with another band member, Peter Knight, he produced an electric folk opera *The King of Elfland's Daughter* (1977). This was based upon the book of the same title by Lord Dunsany (an author in the vein of Machen and a great influence upon H. P. Lovecraft). Dunsany's book is, without doubt, a modern classic- a memorable reinterpretation of traditional faery themes, which believes in magic and at the same time gently mocks human belief in it. The text feels almost ageless in its stately pace and singular phrasing- which are a joy to read.

The 1977 record featured contributions from, amongst others, Welsh folk singer and Eurovision entrant Mary Hopkin (playing the king's daughter, Lirazel), Herbie Flowers, who played bass with T. Rex and David Bowie, blues musician Alexis Korner (in the role of the Troll) and actor Christopher Lee, star of (amongst so many films) *The Wicker Man*, who acted as the album's narrator and took the part of the King of Elfland. The record's cover was designed by Jimmy Cauty, later to be a member of *The Orb* and then the *KLF*.

The entire album is short (especially by the standards of the genre), running for only thirty-five minutes in total. It comprises nine tracks, which are performed in a variety of styles- rock, acoustic and orchestral. Some of the songs are named after characters in the story (*Lirazel* and *Alveric's Journey Through Elfland*), some borrow from Dunsany's text

(*Beyond the Fields We Know* or *The Rune of the Elf King*) and some are descriptive.  The entire vocal score can be viewed on the *MainlyNorfolk* web pages.[55]

The *AllMusic* website is fairly devastating in its assessment of the album.[56]  To begin with, its timing, just as punk entered its ascendancy, was poor: the public's indulgence towards 'concept albums' had virtually evaporated, having been sorely tried in previous years by *Yes* triple albums and Rick Wakeman's solo work- *Journey to the Centre of the Earth* and *The Six Wives of Henry VIII.*  Not only was the record entirely out of synch with the *zeitgeist,* but it boasted "a star-studded cast that omitted any current stars" and, in consequence, garnered very poor sales and no publicity.

> "the album was utterly preposterous... [there were] a succession of bludgeoning miscasts [such as] a frankly puzzled Alexis Korner [which combined to] hopelessly overwhelm Mary Hopkin's lithesome appearances as the heroine, Lirazel, and P.P. Arnold's spellbinding witch."

The music is condemned as functional and perfunctory- and yet, "still there is a charm to the affair... a Quixotic valour, perhaps, derived from flying so hard against the prevailing winds that it deserves your attention for sheer gall alone." That, combined with a good story very well told, may be sufficient to rescue the album from complete oblivion.

Others have been more generous.  At the time (and very surprisingly, given that it generally championed punk) the music paper *Sounds* wrote that "Contrary to expectations, the two former *Steeleye Span* members did not deliver a folk-rock album, but a kind of folk opera... with refreshingly poppy to

---

[55]

https://mainlynorfolk.info/steeleye.span/records/kingofelflandsdaughter.html.

[56] https://www.allmusic.com/album/king-of-elflands-daughter-mw0000850988.

heart-breaking gems in the style of the 1960s, souped up with strings and brass…" The vocalists performed "in a dramatic recitative that Verdi would have enjoyed- and all of this in a refreshingly uncomplicated way…"

In the present day, the *Green Man* blog still admires the skill with which the essence of the story has been retained whilst editing it into album format. The plot is well paced and retains much of the darkness of Dunsany's authentically dark Faery. The reviewer felt that all characters were well played.[57]

## A Midsummer Night's Happening

We'll conclude this chapter with by collecting together songs and albums that take their theme from Shakespeare's *Midsummer Night's Dream,* the quintessential faery play. Some references to the drama are fairly superficial, as in the title of *Barclay James Harvest's* seventh studio album from 1976, *Octoberon,* the cover artwork of which is probably the only faery thing about it. The same is the case for the band's 1971 song, 'Galadriel' which sounds highly promising- as Mike Barnes has observed it is "one of the few [songs] in the entire progressive rock canon that references J. R. R. Tolkien." However, it seems "to have little to do with the elfin princess." This is quite true- it is essentially just a love song for a young flower-child, who "comes up with the morning sun/ And tells me life has just begun." Other artists of the time showed a deeper knowledge of Faery and legend, though, and made greater use of it too.[58]

The first track on the first side of *Pink Floyd's* debut album, *Piper at the Gates of Dawn,* is the song 'Astronomy Domine.'

---

[57] https://agreenmanreview.com/music-2/bob-johnson-and-pete-knights-the-king-of-elflands-daughter/
[58] Barnes, *New Day Yesterday*, 257; John Godfrey, BJH's original keyboard player, left to form *The Enid* who were mentioned earlier. Their output has been marked by literary references, to John Keats, Shakespeare and to Robert Graves' *The White Goddess.*

It's been called 'space rock' and there is a mention of Dan Dare as well as this strangely confused line- "Jupiter and Saturn, Oberon, Miranda and Titania/ Neptune, Titan, stars can frighten," in which planets and characters from *Midsummer Night's Dream* and *The Tempest* (but no stars) are listed almost haphazardly.[59]

Two years later, in 1969, folk duo *The Sallyangie* released their first and only album, *The Children of the Sun.* The group comprised siblings Sally and Mike Oldfield, whom we've met before; the second track on the second side was the song *Midsummer Night's Happening,* a dream-like evocation of a ball in a country mansion that seems to be set in a vaguely aristocratic and medieval environment (with mentions of knights, ladies, maidens and lords) and which also cites Shakespeare's play more or less directly. Puck is commanded to squeeze juice from a magic flower (as in the play) and the refrains call on the faery king and queen: "Come to the Ball my love, sip sweet ambrosia/ Trip in the forest Titania my love;" "Come my pretty Oberon trip, trip/ Come and sing a summer song. As mentioned earlier, *The Strawbs* also sang about Titania that same year in 'Or Am I Dreaming?'

In 1974 German progressive rockers *Lucifer's Friend* released the track 'Thus Spoke Oberon' on their album *Banquet.* It seems to bear the stamp of Led Zeppelin's 'Stairway to Heaven,' featuring a Misty Mountain Queen who has discovered a hidden and "wonderful world... Flowers adorn the morning air." There is the same sense of wistful loss and pastoral peace, too:

> "And thus, spoke Oberon, we'll fly the evening sky
> Together hand in hand we'll let the days go by
> From April Fool to summer wheels have spun around."

---

[59] For more on both Oberon and Titania, see my *Famous Faeries,* 2020.

All this is set against a delightful melody and a classical/ jazz-rock backing with piano, strings and luscious layered vocal harmonies.

We leap then to 1981, and the album *Mask* by Northampton's goth pioneers *Bauhaus*. The song, *The Hollow Hills,* appears to echo lines from Fiona Macleod's *The Immortal Hour.* The lyric is rich in symbolism: the song warns against the invasion of "Ancient earth work, fort and barrow," especially at Yuletide; the penalty will be death for those who violate the "hollow hills/ That music hold and Oberon fill."
If any mortal is foolish enough to ignore the "baleful sounds and wild voices" and proceeds to violate the "sanctity of supermen's hills," witches and goblins are guaranteed to make them "lament and repent." All this is set to a slow, dissonant and brooding track full of menace.

*Midsummer Night's Dream* is still name-checked by artists today, as in the Australian rock band *Jupiter Revival's* 2011 song, 'Oberon's Son.' The lyrics must surely come from a wider reading than just the famous play: for instance, the reference to "mad Robin's pranks" nods to the text *Robin Goodfellow, His Mad Pranks and Merry Jests* of 1639. Perhaps, therefore, they were correct when US metal band *Metal Church* declared Oberon to be the god of heavy metal in their 1984 track, 'Metal Church.'

# The Eighties & After

Prog rock was an ideal genre within which to compose and perform fantasy and folklore-based songs. The arrival of punk and then new wave from 1976 created an environment increasingly hostile to such subjects: they fitted neither the style of the new music nor its chosen focus upon the real life of its audience. Nevertheless, after an initial period of abeyance, supernatural themes resurfaced in popular music.

## Literary Faeries

An awareness of literature has continued to provide a route by which faery themes, more or less explicitly, enter popular music. A very good example is the 2011 album by *The Waterboys*, titled *An Appointment with Mr Yeats*. This sets fourteen of W. B. Yeats' poems to music, amongst which are 'The Hosting of the Shee' and 'The Faery's Last Song.' This interest in Yeats was far from new: the band's 1988 album *Fisherman's Blues* had set the poet's changeling verse, 'The Stolen Child' to music and there are further faery mentions in 1993's 'Glastonbury Song' (of course) and in 'I know she's in the building' (an "elfin queen" with "firm and supple breast").

Toyah Wilcox also quoted poetry in her 1983 track 'Dreamscape.' The song's refrain, "Come to the dreamscape/ The horns of elfin land are calling you" borrows very clearly from Lord Tennyson's *The Splendour Falls*: "The horns of Elfland faintly blowing," perhaps by way of Lord Dunsany- not just *The King of Elfland's Daughter* but several of his short stories as well- *The Bird of the Difficult Eye*, *Miss Cubbidge and the Dragon of Romance* and *Carcassonne*- all of which use similar phrases.

## Girly Faeries

"I'm a fairy/ I sparkle..."[60]

Conventional conceptions of Faery have not, predictably, left the mainstream. *The Moody Blues'* 1999 album *Strange Times* included the song, 'My Little Lovely' whose title alone indicates its content and tone. The song seems to be addressed to a little girl who's perhaps about to go to sleep, so there's talk of dreams, angels and wizards, alongside the assurance that:

> "Fairy tales sometimes come true-
> Use fairy dust and pixie glue,
> Then all the love will stick to you..."

Of course, little girls love pink faery dresses, unicorns and wands, and what parent (or grandparent) wouldn't indulge them? John Martyn's *Fairy Tale Lullaby* (from 1967) is very similar, promising the little girl dreams of:

> "the magic dancing wood...
> ... where the goblins are all good,
> I will take you where the elves and pixies sing
> And I will take you 'round the magic fairy ring."

On a par too, is Paul McCartney's glutinous 'Children, Children' from his 1978 album *London Town*:

> "I know where there's a fairy
> Who will invite us all to tea-
> But she won't let me in alone
> You'll have to come with me."

The tension that can exist between an interest in magic and the supernatural, and our somewhat instinctive tendency to think of glittery faery wings on elastic, lies behind 'A Cloak of Elvenkind' by late '90s alternative band, *Marcy Playground*. Before the *Lord of the Rings* gave elves a popular status as

---

[60] *Alisha's Attic,* 'Are You Jealous?' 1998.

cool and heroic, an interest in the supernatural was something to be hidden:

> "A cloaking robe of elven kind
> Hangs in my wardrobe behind
> All those things that mother
> Said were proper for a boy…"

A fascination for spells and books is not suitable for boys (at least, in the years before Harry Potter) and, for that matter, society still expects girls to grow out of their passions for kittens and faeries after puberty. Chrissie Hynde reflected upon this fondly and nostalgically in 'Bird of Paradise' (1981):

> "When I was a little girl
> With clay horses and lambs on the shelf
> I caught frogs in ditches, listened for elves,
> My friends and I had a world unto ourselves
> No grownups could find us…"[61]

True to their nature, Manchester's *The Fall* took a bracingly bitter view of the source of much of this sentimentalising of folklore. Their track 'Spoilt Victorian Child' from 1985's *This Nation's Saving Grace* attacks the flower fairies and all such nursery rhyme mythologising:

> "Past trees the fairies are flying-
> Past trees with rose bushes in:
> The child was spoilt Victorian."

Vocalist Mark E. Smith's attitude was only to be expected, perhaps: just the year before he had sung (over what is essentially the chord progression of *Bauhaus'* 'Bela Lugosi is Dead')- "No never, no never no more/ Will I trust the elves of Dunsimore."[62]

---

[61] *The Pretenders,* from the album *Pretenders II.*
[62] 'Elves,' *The Wonderful and Frightening World of the Fall,* 1984. Dunsimore does not exist; the dedicated Fall lyrics website

Adult cynicism and rejection of fantasy was displayed too by singer songwriter Lisa Germano. Her work has always dealt with issues of mental health and failing relationships, so it was entirely in character for her to sing in 2006 "Fairies everywhere/ I don't even like 'em/ I don't even care."[63]

Standing in equally stark contrast to any cloying romanticisation was the indie band, *Grim Faeries,* who believed in faeries- but not as our friends. The band formed in 1998 and released one album, *Disenchanted Forest,* in 2001; their stage-show featured malignly caricatured faery silhouettes as a backdrop and their song, 'Faery Rade' displayed a sound knowledge of traditional faery lore and its darker mood. The faeries warn of taking vengeance for damage to a faery mound ("If you desecrate, we will retaliate"); the least they threaten is classic faery sanction of pinching, but it could be much worse- a home might be burned to the ground. Listeners are advised to wear a cross to protect themselves, but they're warned at the same time that little will deflect the rade:

> "Hide your children, lock your doors,
> Scatter salt around your floors,
> Feel the fear in the air-
> The faerie raid is getting near."

The other reaction to the relentless miniaturisation and trivialisation of faery-kind was that of Lemmy, bassist with *Motörhead.* '(Don't Need) Religion' forcefully rejects all forms and degrees of superstition:

> "I don't need no Santy Claus
> And I don't believe in fairies no more."

---

http://annotatedfall.doomby.com/ speculates that it is a conflation of Macbeth's Dunsinane and Dunsmore, the name of several British settlements.

[63] Lisa Germano, 'In the Land of Fairies,' from *In the Maybe World,* 2006.

In Lemmy's opinion, rock and roll was the only true religion. Curiously, perhaps, *The Who's* bassist John Entwistle appears already to have recorded a direct riposte to this in his 1971 piano ballad 'I Believe in Everything':

"I believe in everything
Cause that's the simplest way for me to be…
… fairies at the bottom of the garden
… goblins, ghouls and witches
Things that go bump in the night."

## Nature Faeries

Fortunately, as we shall soon see, Entwistle was in fact far from being alone in his persistent and unshakeable belief.[64] As observed earlier, cinema gave Tolkien's fables of Middle Earth mainstream glamour, leading to an explosion of fantasy subjects within the most unlikely of genres, heavy metal (see later).

The public embrace of dwarves and elves also encouraged other bands to sing about aspects of Faery that had not attracted public attention previously, such as their role in fighting environmental degradation and climate change. The Dutch symphonic rock band *Within Temptation* released an album in 2001 called *Mother Earth*. In line with the record's title, the song 'Perfect Harmony' envisaged a child born and raised in a forest, sheltered and protected by woodland creatures who become his family:

"Ancient spirits of the forest
Made him king of elves and trees
He was the only human being
Who lived in harmony-
In perfect harmony."

[64] *Motorhead*, from *Iron Fist,* 1982; Entwistle, from *Smash Your Head Against the Wall*, 1971.

Somewhat along the same lines is the song, 'Trows Kind' by Italian folk-metal band *Elvenking*. They identify the good "light" elves of Nordic tradition with the ancient oak trees and describe how:

> "Deep in the woods,
> They're dressed with the fruits of earth-
> Arcane adorers of the roots."

However, these forest elves face pressure from humans that is likely to drive them out of their forest realms.  We shall discuss *Elvenking* again later, but the idea of identity between faes and nature is an important strand of contemporary belief, one that has doubtless been strengthened by Tolkien's vision of woodland dwelling elves (for which, see too *Elvenking*'s 'Banquet of Bards' which takes place amidst ancient oaks, willows and autumn forests).[65]

Very similar is the track 'Eldritch Sorcery and Faery Runes' by Viking folk metal band *Folkearth*.  The lyrics address the "Spirit of the ash tree/ Dweller in the oak," offering to dryads in "pagan forests primeval" a sacrifice of song at "an altar of yew."  There are elven runes in Fangorn's palace, rings of stone, gnarled boughs and a whole mystical realm to which "Trees lively welcome me…" [66]  Likewise, Hungarian folk duo *The Moon and Nightspirit* take us to "ancient forests/ The sylvan abode of faeries and fauns" who are the "steadfast guardians of edenic times." The singer pleads: "Let us return to the garden amaranthine/ Let us leave this sad and grey world."  Forests are a paradise, sacred, magical and alive.

The close relationship between faeries and the processes and cycles of nature is also brought out in the song 'Ostara' by Lisa Thiel.  Ostara is the Germanic goddess of Spring, who

---

[65] See my *Faeries in the Natural World,* 2021.
[66] From the 2004 album, *Nordic Poem;* see too 'Domain of Darksome Ravens' and 'In Blessed Days' from the same album.

was known to the Anglo-Saxons as Eostre, giving us our present word 'Easter.' The goddess is celebrated in a track on Thiel's 2005 album, *The Circle of the Seasons,* as both the 'Maiden' and 'Crone.' The return of fresh life to the earth is the 'Healing of the Green' and is explicitly linked to the nature spirits: "Praise to the Spring… We honour ourselves and all the fairies and elves."

## The Medieval Baebes

As a vocal group dedicated to recording modern versions of old songs, or setting old poems to music, the all-female *Medieval Baebes* have necessarily incorporated a good deal of faery material into their repertoire. Traditional instruments, especially recorders, are a feature of their music, alongside their vocal harmonies.

Their contemporary renditions of folk staples have included the Scots ballad 'Tam Lin'- which has also been recorded by *Fairport Convention* and by Sandy Denny. On the same album, *Mirabilis* (2005), there feature an adaptation of James Hogg's 'Kilmeny' as well as the Manx rhyme 'Lhiannan Shee' (a faery lover). On the 2009 album *Illumination* the Baebes adapted another faery poem, John Keats' classic, 'La Belle Dame Sans Merci,' which *Penda's Fen,* Marianne Faithful and Loreena McKennitt have all interpreted as well. The *Baebe's* album *Undrentide,* released in 2000, incorporated an abbreviated form of the medieval poem 'Sir Orfeo,' which formed the title track. The album also includes the 'Dance of the Trolls' and a version of William Dunbar's poem 'In secreit place, this hinder nicht,' a verse that refers to the fairy bird, the cuckoo, and to the Scots Faery called Mirry-land (albeit not in this version).[67]

The *Baebes* take traditional texts and set them to contemporary music. American singer song writer Emilie Autumn did almost the opposite: her poem, *Alas the Knight,* is

---

[67] See my *Faeries and the Natural World,* Green Magic, 2021.

very deliberately written in archaic diction (thee/ unto/ dwelleth) and is addressed to a faery knight, one of a "distant, beauteous race," whom she has summoned into our world.[68]

## Ritchie Blackmore

Former lead guitarist of heavy rock bands *Deep Purple* and *Rainbow,* since 1995 Blackmore has taken a turn into acoustic folk-rock, working with his partner Candice Night as *Blackmore's Night.*[69] This medieval inspired balladry inevitably involved him in faery themes, much as it had *Led Zeppelin* and others before and since.

Instrumental tracks by Blackmore include *The Wild Dance of the Fairies,* whilst *Faerie Queen- Faerie Dance,* from the 2006 album *Village Lanterne,* gives a good idea of the vision of Faery presented. The fairy queen sits on a tiny golden chair within a flower on a hill. She is a nature spirit, ruling over woodland plants in the same vein as Titania:

> "It is in her breath
> That the wind does blow
> It is in her heart
> As pure as winter snow
> It is in her tears
> Crystal raindrops fall
> And within her years
> That she is in us all..."

Very much as in 'Stairway to Heaven,' there is an undercurrent of sadness and dissatisfaction. The narrator of the song longs to see the queen, but knows that a brief

---

[68] From Autumn's 2001 poetry collection, *Your Sugar Sits Untouched*, and also set to music on CD.
[69] Trivia note: Ronnie James Dio, vocalist in *Rainbow,* began his career in a group called *The Electric Elves*, subsequently *The Elves* and then *Elf*. Their 1972 album *Elf* has a leering elven male on the cover; other than that, though, it is quite elf-free.

glimpse of her is all that s/he may get before the faery vanishes.  There is a painful sense of transience: "We are one/ Fading with the setting sun..."

Blackmore has inspired other musicians to follow his lead. *Elflore*, for example, who hail originally from Texas and Canada, proclaim themselves to be a medieval folk-rock band in the style of *Blackmore's Night*.

## Modern Folk

Folk-rock band *Renaissance* entered the 1980s with an updated electronic sound but, despite the synthesisers, their subject matter remained resolutely traditional- as 1981's *Fairies Living at the Bottom of the Garden* demonstrates.  It is full of significant fae elements: a rowan tree, a "faerie ring untouched by time" and a child-like fear of abduction by the Good Neighbours.  The chorus, "Faeries living at the bottom of the garden/ Someone's calling, I am falling, falling..." inevitably puts one in mind of Rose Fyleman's 1918 poem 'There are Fairies at the Bottom of my Garden,' which was recorded by Bea Lillie in 1934.  The tone of the original is much gentler and kinder, though, with no hint of any threat of being taken by 'Them.'

Akin to these songs is 'Back In' by American-Russian songwriter Regina Spektor.  She claims to have secret and arcane knowledge of an enchanted realm in the past when the world was at peace; she can "speak in the ancient tongue" and is, to all intents and purposes, identified with the faeries:

> "Six faeries spinning in the breeze,
> six sisters of the sky;
> And now imagine if you please,
> the seventh one was I."

London Irish band *The Pogues* have covered Irish folk staples and have composed their own convincingly authentic classics as well.  Their breakneck reel, *The Haunting,* from 1993, is one such; a man cycling to a dance gets caught by a downpour and takes shelter amongst "the trees at the old fairy fort."  Standing watching the torrents fall, "a voice it says- 'dirty ould night'."  There is no speaker to be seen; the man flees, despite the weather and is terrified "for weeks and weeks after with nerves a disaster."  Although the song's title suggests ghosts, a passing knowledge of folklore will assure us that those "burial chambers" beneath the cyclist's feet contain more than the spirits of ancient warriors.  The fairies and the dead have a longstanding and complex relationship.[70]

Traditional classics can continue to evolve as well.  *Fairport Convention,* on their 1970 album, *Hark! The Village Wait,* recorded a version of a folk staple, 'Copshawholme Fair' which was originally written by the 'labouring class poet,' David Anderson, in 1793.  In 2011 the German folk rock band *Faun* recorded a version entitled 'The Market Song,' featuring an added element of menace, a subtle hint of faery abduction and the refrain:

> "You came a long way, you travelled for so long.
> Now rest your head before the summer's gone,
> Meet us in the sunny fields and meet us in the greenwood deep
> And step in our faerie ring 'cause you'll never ever, ever, be the same again."

Even today, songwriters can still turn anew to the themes (and antiquated diction) of folk-rock.  See, for example, Billy Corgan, originally of the *Smashing Pumpkins,* who in a 2019 song 'Jubilee' sang how:

> "Glow worms spin sails for thy breath
> Our faeries' fairest ship sends a most oft regret
> The virgin ground pounds proud hearts to transience
> As sadness is one

---

[70] See my *Faery,* 2020, 31 or *Beyond Faery,* 2020, 6.

A faerie's strength is in the murk…"

I'm not sure I know exactly what this means, but his heart's in the right place.

Most remarkable of these new incarnations of old material, perhaps, is Marianne Faithfull's 2018 release, 'The Gypsy Faerie Queen,' which was recorded jointly with Nick Cave. The song is voiced by Puck (or Robin Goodfellow) who follows the gypsy faerie queen across the length and breadth of England, existing in the "twilight in-between." The queen no longer talks, but you will hear her:

> "Singing her song, using her wand
> To help and heal the land and the creatures on it.
> She's dressed in rags of moleskin
> And wears a crown of rowan berries on her brow."

The song is delightfully wistful, with its spare instrumentation, and strongly projects a sense of the loving and devoted service of Puck to his monarch. Faithfull's 1967 song, 'Good Guy,' also conveys a more sober and nuanced view of Faery, with its "Fairy castle, stark and black in the moonlight." There is magic, but it may not make you happy.

## Goth and Metal

After the upheavals of new wave, heavy metal re-emerged as a vital force- in the New Wave of British Heavy Metal, as the music papers catchily titled it, and in numerous developments and evolutions since- death metal, extreme metal and so on (see Coda Two). Goth, a fusion of indie and some of the darker elements of seventies heavy rock (the more histrionic moments of *Black Sabbath, Alice Cooper* and *Judas Priest)* also provided a conduit for folk and mythical themes to be explored again.

For example, British goth heroes *The Mission* released 'Deliverance' in 1990, a song that mentions the lady of the lake, the fairy queen, fairy rings, Avalon, Beltane fires and circles of stone. The chorus exhorts us to:

> "Believe in magic,
> Believe in lore, legend and myth,
> And the hand that guides
> In the cunning of hope,
> In the weaving of dreams..."

Another major goth band, *The Cult,* envisaged some sort of cataclysm in Faery in the song 'Ashes and Ghosts' (2001). A sorcerer has taken revenge for a breach of faith, it would appear:

> "I look around the world and see
> The winged waifs powdered on petal dust...
> The assassin's hand has planned
> To pull the wings off every one of us...
> Cracked fairy heads are spinning down...
> You're fading, yeah, you're fading..."

The death of faeries is a subject seldom mentioned, either in folklore or (certainly) in nursery tales. It's refreshing, therefore, to hear this perspective- and it provides us with an introduction to darker visions still.[71]

Extreme metal band *Cradle of Filth* are known for the wide range of literary and mythological references in their rich lyrics, and the song 'Rise of the Pentagram' is no exception. We are introduced to a house of incest where "Blasphemies against Venus were rent." The speaker and his partner undress, then they-

> "haunt fairy groves

---

[71] On faery mortality, see my *Faery Lifecycle,* 2021, c.5 or *Faery,* 2020, 190.

And hot virgin coves
Wherein the promiscuous swam."

The band's song 'Deflowering the Maidenhead, Displeasuring the Goddess,' released in 2015, is a lament over ecocide, a hymn to Queen Catastrophia. The planet is being raped by humanity- by overpopulation, deforestation, pollution and by pandemics (presciently). Mother Earth, Gaia, Cybele, Ishtar, the Goddess, is assaulted, by "the greed that tore Her elvish bodice" and which is now destroying Eden. We are assured that she will take her revenge.[72]

Sex should never be very far from authentic faes, and with the Slovakian black metal band *Ethereal Pandemonium,* this is certainly the case. Their song, 'Last Phoenix Rising' promises "Erotic enchantment in the embrace of crimson dreams" and "bare breasted faeries [who] dance in nocturnal woods."

Magic and mysticism are commoner themes in metal tracks, though. Swedish black metal band *Bathory* invoked witches and "elven stones" in their songs 'Spellcraft Moonfire' and 'Dreaming of Atlantean Spires.' The latter also featured sorcerers, shadow kings and a "black elven sword." Czech folk metal band *Emerald Shine,* on their track 'Autumn Mists' conjure a far gentler scene of sylvan enchantment, with medieval-tinged harps and recorders. We are reassured that the fair folk are not just gone or "waned, mere memories." Walking lost in a misty wood, the band hear sweet music and "just by chance we got into the elven land" and stumbled cross the elven autumn festival:

"Believe it is not a dream
See the Elves dancing among the trees
Singing in the autumn mists…"

---

[72] On the presence of the goddess in *Cradle of Filth*'s work, see my *Aphrodite,* 2021.

The Finnish symphonic metal band, *Nightwish,* in true Tolkien approved fashion, revert to their roots and national mythology on the song 'Elvenpath.' They see "an elvish sight" and (like *Emerald Shine*) hear:

> "music from the deepest forest
> Songs as a seduction of sirens
> The elf-folk are calling me."

The lyrics invoke ancient tribal gods (Tapio, Bearking, Ruler of the Forest and Mielikki) as well as Home Gnome (presumably the Swedish *nisse* or *tomte,* a creature related to the British brownie and hobgoblin) and Bilbo. What's strongest is that sense of yearning for a better past that we met before in *Led Zeppelin*:

> "It's the honesty of these worlds
> Ruled by magic and mighty swords
> That makes my soul long for the past-
> Elvenpath."

The same band's 'Sacrament of Wilderness' mentions more fairy music, the sound of "Dulcet elven-harps from a dryad forest." In fact, one (slightly overwrought) reviewer even described vocalist Johanna Kurkela as sounding like "a female elf singing, very soft and light, just like the whispering of the wind on the leaves of flowers." *Nightwish* have also recorded an *Elven Jig,* an instrumental track with clear Irish or Celtic roots.[73]

All the key elements of this sub-genre of song- forests, wizards, maidens, kings in halls, a virgin princess and the army of the Faery Queen- can also be found within the relentless barrage of the track 'Under the Boughs' by Texan heavy metal band *The Sword.* The same could be said of Newcastle's extreme metal band, *Venom,* whose riff-heavy 'Faerie Tale' is a catalogue of nursery rhyme elements

---

[73] https://metalshockfinland.com/tag/tuomas-holopainen/

clashing with nightmare imagery- as the song warns "The pied piper plays his song/ Come follow to your death." The Swedish heavy metal band, *Lake of Tears*, recorded the far gentler 'Lady Rosenred' in 1997: "There's a faerie in my head and I call her Lady Rosenred/ Why she came there I don't know."[74] Nevertheless, we discover bards, green forests and 'dragon fairies' and are invited to "Say will you dream with me tonight, under moonlit skies." Several of the tracks mentioned in this last paragraph seem, to me, to be straying into pure Tolkien territory, which I shall discuss in the next section.

*Inkubus Sukkubus* are a British goth and pagan band; their track 'Goblin Jig' from the album *Beltaine* of 1996 (like *Emerald Shine)* joins the faery people in a dance to rhythmic, hypnotic beat of the bodhran:

"Come and join the dance without delay
Let the faery people lead the way
When their voices call you, you obey..."

This is a benign and celebratory vision. However, in 1998 the band released an album titled *Away with the Faeries.* The track of that name imagines a magic mushroom trip carrying us away to where the fae are singing and dancing. The song provides a concise summary of the conflicting Christian explanations of the origins of the Good Folk: "they were once known as angels from the sky and heaven/ But now they are known as devils, demons, alien monsters" and the track is prepared to be ambivalent and honest about the experience of meeting them: "Let them fill your dreams with wonder, fever, pain and passion..." The faery queen is seen, seated on a toadstool, a "faery harlot [who] will lead if you will follow/ Down the road that leads to sorrow." The psylocibin can open the doors of perception, then, but it may be a "sacred poison" that the human regrets consuming.

---

[74] See too the choirs of winged faeries in the band's song 'The Path of The Gods (Upon The Highest Mountain, Part 2).'

108

*Inkubus Sukkubus* took their name from a song by German goth pioneers, *Xmal Deutschland.* That band's exact contemporaries, *Einstürzende Neubaten* showed similar supernatural interests, their song *Salamandrina* describing the mythical creatures as "Not mermaids, nymphs, sylphs, elves/ Muses or fairies.*"*

Brazilian symphonic metal band, *Lords of Aesir,* combine many elements we have already encountered- a "meadow of warriors," ladies, "music of the forest," magic and "the spells of the elvish night"- within the ambitious operatic sweep of their 2014 song 'Elvish Night.' Whilst their native country is less apt, the group's name serves to remind us how in the Nordic countries one branch of folk-metal has transmuted into a revived Viking music with pagan themes. These may be out and out metal, attempted recreations of Viking music (such as *Wardruna,* whose tracks are used on the *Vikings* TV series) or folk tunes fused with a modern beat.

Exemplars of this trend include *Therion,* a symphonic metal band from Sweden, whose 2001 album *Secret of the Runes* drew its ideas from Norse mythology. The track 'Ljosalfheim' (the realm of the Light Elves) describes the:

> "Solar glare from Lord Frej- The Shining One-
> In Ljosalfheim he's king of elves;
> High above the rainbow and in the tarn
> Deep in the wood you'll find the elves."

Other artists who have drawn upon the ancient sagas of elves include German singer Andrea Haugen's project *Hagalaz Runedance* (songs such as 'A Tale of Fates,' 'Alav' and 'When the Falcon Flies') and fellow Germans *Falkenbach,* a Viking metal band, whose songs are even sung in Norse, for example 'I Nattens Stilta' and 'Hava Mal.'

*Thyrfing,* a Viking metal band from Sweden, pair the elves and the valkyries on 'Breaking of Serenity.' The one-man Swedish black metal project, *Diabolical Masquerade,* make "Blackheim the father of all the Black Elves" on the 1996 album, *Ravendusk in my Heart. Aeternus* is a 'blackened death metal band' from Bergen. Their song, 'Raven and Blood,' invokes the ancient learning of the *Edda* and the "elves of wisdom." The *Poetic Edda* also underlies the song *Alfablot* (Elvish Sacrifice) by extreme metal band *Enslaved*, also from Bergen, a track which is a suitably violent evocation of a boar offered to the elves to hasten the return of spring.

Finally, despite this persistent bias towards Norse/ Germanic myth, other traditions are addressed. Elves and dwarves appear in 'Song of Taliesin,' by Düsseldorf's *Suidakra*, a German melodic death metal band who refreshingly looked to ancient Welsh and British myth for their lyrical inspiration.

# Lost in Tolkien

"Will there be fairies, or things to fear?"[75]

The music and art of each generation cannot help but reflect, most of the time, the prevailing perceptions of contemporary culture. This is especially true of faeries. Our view now of the faery realm is one that has been substantially shaped by the work of two men: the books of author J. R. R. Tolkien and the films based on those books by Peter Jackson. They have instilled in us a vision of elves and dwarves which it may take us many decades to displace.

J. R. R. Tolkien's books, *Lord of the Rings, The Hobbit, The Silmarillion* and others have already been mentioned several times. Their mixture of myth, fantasy, horror and folk tradition has been enormously influential upon music, film and art since the late 1960s, as I already suggested when discussing *Led Zeppelin*. That band's songs wore their influences fairly lightly; the same can be said of *Black Sabbath*, whose 1970 track 'The Wizard' is reputed to be about Gandalf, but which is general enough to apply to any wizard you may care to mention.

The link between Middle Earth and music is deepened further still by the fact that Tolkien himself saw music and song as fundamental to his mythology. The *Ainulindalë* ('The Music of the Ainur' in the Elvish language Quenya) is the story of the creation of the world that is found in the first part of *The Silmarillion*. The immortal *Ainur* are the children of the deity Ilúvatar; they are taught the art of music, which becomes their mission. They sing, either alone or in small groups, on themes given to them by Ilúvatar, with the aim of creating a universal harmony.

---

[75] 'Fly' by *Blind Guardian*.

Since the early 1970s, many artists have borrowed far more directly from Tolkien than *Led Zep* and *Sabbath*, going beyond homage, sometimes, to what resembles the actual sound-tracking of the books. There are numerous examples of bands and songs whose debts to Tolkien are extremely apparent. Needless to say, perhaps, elves and goblins (amongst other such beings) abound. A sign of the early impact of Tolkien's books on later sixties 'serious' rock may be judged from one small feature of the scene: venue names. Mention has already been made of *Middle Earth* club in London's Covent Garden where John Peel DJ'd; in Wimbledon there was the *Hobbit's Garden*, where *Genesis, Roxy Music, Hawkwind, Pink Fairies* and *Barclay James Harvest*- amongst others- all appeared. Many of their punters would have been reading the underground magazine, *Gandalf's Garden*- or visiting the publisher's shop of the same name in Chelsea.

It must be emphasised that Tolkien's influence upon visions of Faery is quite unique and personal to him. He was, without question, well versed in British faerylore, but he was a professor of literature, so he drew upon sources as varied as the Anglo-Saxon *Beowulf,* the Middle English *Sir Gawain and the Greene Knight,* Arthurian romance, the Finnish *Kalevala,* Greek myth, Norse legends and sagas, the Irish myths of the *Tuatha de Danaan* and continental Germanic folk stories and legends. Whilst his dwarves and trolls are clearly Germanic, his elves seem to descend from Celtic roots. There is much that is familiar to English readers in Middle Earth, but there is little, perhaps, that is specifically or distinctly British- unless we liken Smaug to the barrow dwelling dragon in the land of the Geats in *Beowulf* (and *they* are, in point of fact, Danish).

One other preliminary remark must be to observe the incredible range of artistic responses to the Tolkien's work. There are attempts to recreate medieval style musics that would be 'appropriate' to the cultures he imagined; there are folk and folk-rock interpretations and, at the other extreme, there is sonically challenging metal that is as far from the soothing sylvan sounds of pipes and harps as it's possible to imagine.  The former may evoke the elves; the latter are highly suitable to the brutal hand to hand brawling of armoured warriors.

## Elder Days

As early as 1969, Jack Bruce, bass player in the rock supergroup *Cream,* recorded the impressionistic acoustic track 'To Isengard.' In the following year, the Dane Bo Hansonn released *Sagan om ringen,* an album that received an international distribution as *Music Inspired by Lord of the Rings* in 1972.  Mike Barnes has observed, cruelly but not unfairly, that whilst the music was evocative, the cover for this record conjured up thoughts of pictures of the book's characters that "disappointingly, were depicted in a way that didn't look anything like you had imagined."  There are actually three versions of the cover.  *Sagan om ringen* appeared with a brightly coloured scene of a volcano and Sauron's tower that looks like a German Expressionist work. The original English language cover, by Jane Furst, is quite surrealist: a hand holding the ring is extended over a stylised landscape in which various figures are arranged.  Mounted knights battle ring-wraiths, their poses reminiscent of Paolo Uccello's *St George and the Dragon* while, for some not immediately explicable reason, a prone figure closely resembling Mantegna's famous *Lamentation of Christ* lies dead.  The cover of the 1977 reissue is a Roger Deane style scene of orcs and a dragon (in fact painted by Rodney Matthews).[76]

Equalling Hansson in ambition was late 1960s American occult rock band *Coven,* whose song 'Elfstone' is essentially a short summary of the whole of *Lord of the Rings.*  In 1974, British prog rockers *Camel* celebrated an elf maiden mentioned in *Lord of the Rings* and the wizard Gandalf in their nine-minute Moog driven track 'Nimrodel / The Procession /

---

[76] Barnes, *New Day Yesterday,* 356.

The White Rider.' Like many, the band had been reading Tolkien at the time and were looking for a text to set to music-although they ultimately chose Paul Gallico's *Snow Goose*. The mythical interest was present in their music nonetheless: their 1973 track 'Mystic Queen' imagined her "Riding in her limousine/ Over hills and over dales till morning"- an odd combination of modernity and Led Zep medievalism. The latter tone got stronger in the lines that followed: "We'll find some colours you can wear/ Colours that you've only seen while sleeping."

We'll merely note the title of *Argent*'s song, 'Lothlorien' from 1971, before proceeding to the 1975 track, *Rivendell*, recorded by Canadian progressive rock band *Rush* for their album *Fly by Night*. There's very little need to say what it's about or where they got the idea:

> "Elfin songs and endless nights
> Sweet wine and soft relaxing lights
> Time will never touch you
> Here in this enchanted place."

The song itself would appear to owe a good deal to *Stairway to Heaven*, being performed on acoustic guitar with a synthesised accompaniment. It's a soothing, slow and balladlike track well suited to its subject.

Sally Oldfield, sister of Mike, released the sixteen minute long 'Songs of the Quendi' on her 1978 debut album *The Water Bearer*. It's a curious track that begins as a salsa ('Night Theme'), then segues from the clearly Native American 'Wampum Song' into 'Nenya' (the white ring), retaining a sprightly 'American Indian' beat. Nevertheless, we're definitely in Middle Earth, as the chorus makes clear: "Three rings for the elven kings under the sky! Wrought of star-fire!" Elvish words and names are scattered throughout the song- for example, a list of elven tribes, the *laiquendi* (green elves), *moriquendi* (the dark elves) and the *calaquendi* (the light elves).[77]

In retrospect, Mike Barnes has remarked upon the paucity of prog rock tracks and albums from the 1970s that were inspired by Tolkien. This seems especially surprising given the widespread popularity of his work and, as Barnes notes acutely, "the fact that it referenced an imagined and unheard musical tradition, with numerous songs laid out in the text..." As we shall discover, more recent artists have not overlooked these possibilities.[78]

## "Do not go to the elves for counsel"?

In more recent decades, a great deal of music that is even more seriously steeped in Middle Earthly imagery and allusions to elven things has been composed. A first example of such works is the following: 'To be honest' by *Luthien,* an Argentinian band whose name is taken from the elf-maiden Luthien Tinuviel, a major character in the *Silmarillion.* Luthien also appears in songs composed by Russian power metal group *Icewind Tales,* by *Clamavi de Profundis, Karliene, The Middle Earth Band* (for whom see later) and by Irish folk metal band *Cruachan,* who also deal with elvish issues in their song 'The Fall of Gondolin'.

Tolkien has extensively influenced the Finnish heavy metal band *Battlelore*, who refer to elves in 'Journey to Undying Lands,' (amongst several other songs)[79] from their 2002 album *Where the Shadows Lie* (a title which is itself taken from Tolkien's poem on the three rings of power: "in the land of Mordor, where the shadows lie"). *Battlelore*'s song 'Grey Wizard' is about Gandalf, predictably, as are the tracks 'Dawn

---

[77] Here Tolkien has borrowed directly from the Norse *Edda*, which describes the *svart-alfar* and *myrkalfar* (the light and dark elves).
[78] Barnes, *New Day Yesterday,* 356.
[79] *Battlelore* also sing about elves in 'Journey to Undying Lands,' 'The Great Gathering,' 'Into the New World,' 'Attack of the Orcs,' 'A Touch of Green and Gold' and 'Khaza-Dum.'

Take You All' by *Thorr-Axe* and *Attacker's* 'Battle at Helm's Deep.'

The same line, "Where the Shadows Lie" also provided a song title for the Cleveland-based dark ambient synth project *Agahnim*, from their 2017 album *Ethereal Requiems at the Black Gate* (the gate is the northern entrance to Mordor, by the way). Elves also feature in 'Through Elven Woods and Dwarven Mines' amongst several other tracks by Swedish power metal band *Dragonland*.[80] They are to be found, too, on *Morgana Lefay's* 'Lord of the Rings' (naturally) and on 'Autumn of Lothlorien' by the Finnish black metal band *Avathar*. There are elves mentioned too on the track 'Nightshade Forests' from the third album, *Dol Guldu,r* by Vienna's black metal band *Summoning* ("Immortal maiden elven-wise... dance with me");[81] on 'The Fellowship' by US heavy metal band *Sindar* and in several songs by *Indomitable* from Indianapolis, including 'Raze the Village' and 'Plot of Death.' From Bristol band *Noctule* we have the song 'Elven Sword;' note, too, the tracks 'The Silmarillion' from Nashville's *Regdar and the Fighters*; 'The Eagle and the Child' by Merseyside's *Steel Forge* and Czech band *Emerald Shine's* 'Elven King.'

German power metal band *Blind Guardian* refer to Tolkien's clan of elves, the Noldor, as well as to the elven king, on their album *Nightfall in Middle Earth* (which dramatises events in *The Silmarillion)* and in several other tracks such as 'Time Stands Still (At the Iron Hill);' Gandalf too merits a mention from them in their song 'Majesty.'[82] The band's drummer, Thomen Stauch, was also involved in a side project called *Savage Circus* whose power metal ballad, 'Beyond Reality' imagined how:

---

[80] See too *Dragonland*'s 'Ride for Glory' and 'Battle of the Ivory Plains.'
[81] See forest elves as well in the *Summoning's* tracks 'Across the Streaming Tide' and 'The Forest of Dol Guldur.'
[82] See elves too in *Blind Guardian's* songs 'Last Candle,' 'Dark Passage,' 'Lord of the Rings' and 'Bard's Song.'

"In the woods the elves are calling-
Wonderland, when night is falling…
Bringing on the wildest dreams
The fairy tales and magic things
Oh, dreamland, it's calling my name…"

With harpsichord, piano and layered vocals, it's easy to see a debt to *Queen*. Elves feature too in 'The Silent Forest' and in several others tracks on the 2004 album *Scroll of Stone* by Romanian power metal band *Magica*.[83] Both dragons and elves appear in the song 'Of Wars in Osyrhia' by French symphonic metal band *Fairyland* and- lastly- on 'King of the Distant Forest' by the Swedes *Mithotyn*.

Many metal bands deal generally in fantasy and so with elves, dwarves and the like. Some- as already witnessed- quote much more directly from Tolkien's best-known works. Italian folk metal band *Elvenking,* for example, wrote a song called 'Oakenshield' and regularly refer to elvendom, elven legions and the elven king in their songs- see, for instance, 'Banquet of Bards' and, much more remarkably, 'Trows' Kind.' This track from the band's 2006 album *Winter Wake* is a unique catalogue of British folklore, from the Shetland trows "henking" at a dance, taking in southern Scottish Redcaps who are "greedy for silver and gold" to witches in the form of hares. The song is a lament for a fading faery kind:

"Through years and centuries,
Through myth and poetry
Our race's slowly dying
In the heart of mankind."

At the same time, though, the lyrics are not sentimental about fae nature: they are

---

[83] See too 'Wormwood' and 'Bittersweet Nightshade' on their album *Lightseeker.*

"Nymphs of dark and lust- Fairy of bad fate!"  Although it is reported that-

> "Somebody tells he has seen
> Some of the little ones
> Some even that have talked with them
> So nice and handsome…"

- overall, the band seem to be under no illusions about the perilous truth of faery nature: ""Please, don't be such a fool!" Faeries can be highly alluring, tempting humans into ill-advised sexual liaisons: "Desire grows, denial howls/ Your will has gone," but the only likely outcome is enslavement and subjection.

Another illustration of the power of Tolkien comes from the Greek power metal band *Battleroar* whose song 'Narsil (Reforge the Sword)' features the elf Elrond and his home, Rivendell, whilst the band call on the "Elves of Lothlorien" during their track 'Attack of the Orcs.'  This elvish forest realm also gets a mention in 'When Leaves Fall' by Bury heavy rockers *Exist the Fall.*

It should by now come as scant surprise to readers to learn that the Texan band calling themselves *Hobbit* released several Tolkien-themed albums, including *Rockin' in the Shire* from 2001.  The track 'No Doubt and No Expectations' describes Gandalf taking Bilbo Baggins on his great adventure; 'Join the Celebration' includes Rivendell, elves, Treebeard and 'pipeweed.'  Spanish melodic metal band, *Arwen,* managed to cram goblins, witches, unicorns, and a princess who sat "in the light/ of the moon listening to the fairies cry" into their song 'Once Upon a Time.'

*Rivendell* (who were previously known as *Fangorn*) are an Austrian black metal band whose music incorporates a strong folk influence.  As their name might well lead you to anticipate, their song titles include *Aragorn Son of Arathorn, Earendil, Luthien, Mithrandir, Theoden, Misty Mountains, Tinuviel* and (of course) *Rivendell,* the chorus of which is "To Rivendell, where Elves yet dwell/ In glades beneath the misty fell." Lothlorien gets repeated mentions, too, in songs, not least from the Celtic music group *Lothlorien,* who are from New Zealand, but also by Poles *Lugburz* ('Lothlorien- Realm of Night'), in 'Guardians of Lothlorien' by Swedes *Dragon Steel* and in *Mysterium's* 'The Dark Age of Lothlorien.'

Tolkienish tracks from bands who are demonstrably fascinated with Middle Earth- to the extent of naming themselves in the Orcish Black Speech (as is the case with *Lugburz* just mentioned)- are really pretty unremarkable. By way of contrast, the fact that Cliff Richard sang a song about "Galadriel, Spirit of Starlight" will astound many. Nonetheless:

> "She's a light to guide me through the fray...
> Eagle and dove gave birth to thee...
> You are my love and earth to me..."

This track was released on Sir Cliff's 1983 live album, *Dressed for the Occasion,* which was recorded at the Royal Albert Hall with the London Philharmonic Orchestra to mark his twenty-fifth year in the music industry. It seems entirely out of time (as well as out of character) and- to some extent- it was. The tune was originally composed by Hank Marvin and John Farrar and was included on their *Marvin and Farrah* album of 1973. It subsequently formed the B-side to a single, 'Small and Lonely Light' which was issued in 1975. As a tune for acoustic guitar, orchestra and choir, it bears some lineal descent from *Stairway to Heaven* and has layered vocals and other production effects that make it seem pretty hippy and trippy. Rather more what we might have predicted are mentions of 'the lady of the woods' in 'Galadriel' by Russian power trash metal band, *Shadow Host,* 'The Dark Age of Lothlorien' from German melodic death metal band *Mysterium,* 'Princess of the Trees' by Swiss folky-power metal band *Excelsis* and, most uniquely, 'Galadriel's Song' by the Cambodian hard rock band *Drakkar* from their album *Razorblade God* of 2002.

A word on the cover art of this genre of album is probably justified. I described earlier the Renaissance influences detectable in the cover of Bo Hansson's *(Music Inspired by) Lord of the Rings*. Subsequently, two powerful inspirations have shaped the artwork of many albums. Roger Deane came to prominence in the mid-1970s for his work with bands such as *Osibisa* and *Yes,* and his hyper-realist sci-fi style has certainly been adopted for many records. Rather more recently, it seems very clear (again) how pervasive the look of Peter Jackson's films of *Lord of the Rings* has proved, for example in details such as crowns and swords. Viking imagery and symbols probably derived from *Game of Thrones* are also noticeable.

Needless to say, budgets can affect everything. The albums of *Dwarrowdelf,* which will be discussed later, are graced with truly beautiful fantasy landscapes that evoke the work of German Romantic Caspar David Friedrich. By contrast, the cover of *Hobbit's* 'Rockin the Shire' is a grotesque cartoonish caricature.

## Ancient Elvish Books

Collections of stories and myths lie at the core of the histories of Middle Earth- ancient volumes such as the elvish *Golden Books*, the hobbits' *Red Book of Westmarch* and the dwarves' *Book of Mazarbul.* As a result, the creation of *legendaria* has become an idea that has spread from the work of Tolkien not just to other fantasy writers but to lyricists and musicians as well.

For example, *Rhapsody of Fire* are an Italian symphonic power metal band who have gone so far down the Tolkienesque road as to invent their own entire fantasy kingdom. This is a realm populated by elves, wizards and dragon-lords, all of which are described in detail on ambitiously vast orchestral and operatic tracks such as

'Erian's Mystical Rhymes- The White Dragon's Order.' This mythology and the role of elves within it may also be found in other of their songs, such as 'Unholy War Cry,' 'Old Age of Wonders,' 'Dar Kunor' and 'Myth of the Holy Sword.' In truth, so immersed do the band seem to be in fantasy themes, that it would be hard to find a track by this band that does *not* mention the elves. Hardly surprisingly, then, they have been called 'elf metal' by one rock journalist.[84] Fellow Italians *Emyn Muil* drew heavily upon Tolkien's *Silmarillion* for their third release, the epic electronic album *Afar Angathfark* of 2020. Its title is in the Orcish Black Speech, an exclamation meaning 'By the forge of my soul.'

Meanwhile, British epic black metal band *Dwarrowdelf* sing about Aragorn and his elfin lover Arwen amidst raging and soaring guitars on the 2020 album *Evenstar*. The band is the solo studio project of Southampton guitarist Tom O'Dell. His first EP, 2017's *Of Darkened Halls,* was about dwarves, so the follow up in 2018, *The Sons of Fëanor-* and his subsequent releases- which have focussed upon elves, may seem almost inevitable. The third album, *From Beneath the Fells,* describes its sound as "dungeon synth," perhaps a poor term for its harp-like tones. O'Dell has cheerfully labelled himself as a "Tolkien nerd" and has said that the second album was "Tolkien through and through." In addition, he's unashamedly expressed his love of the elves who feature "in most fantasy worlds: they're elegant, they're fierce, they've got awesome hair... this list could go on."[85]

In recent decades, too, American prog rockers *Glass Hammer* have released two Middle Earth themed albums, *The Journey of the Dunadan* (1993) and *The Middle Earth Album* (2001). *Narsilion*, from Barcelona, described themselves as a

---

[84] Other elvish tracks from *Rhapsody* include 'Heart of the Darklands,' 'Heroes of the Waterfall's Kingdom,' 'On the Way to Ainar,' 'Village of Dwarves,' 'Son of Pain,' 'Shadows of Death,' 'Last Angel's Call,' 'Mystic Prophecy of the Demon Knight' and 'Lux Triumphans.'
[85] https://blackmetaldaily.wordpress.com/2018/10/14/.

neoclassical darkwave/ ethereal folk band; their name derives from an elvish lay that's mentioned briefly in *The Silmarillion.* Three of their albums have elvish names, including *Namárië* (2008) and *Elenna Nórë* (2011). 'A Night in Fairyland,' on their debut album *Nerbeleth,* invokes the magic of dancing in moonlit woods- its chorus tells us that it's "time to sing in the land of dreams [and] time to cry for the lost innocence," sentiments familiar from *Led Zeppelin* amongst others. Truly ambitious was the Russian power metal band *Epidemia,* who released an entire concept album and metal opera in 2004. *Elfiyskaya Rukopis* (Elven Manuscript) is an hour-long epic fantasy story, in part derived from *Lord of the Rings.* Another Russian black metal band, *Rakoth,* confirm for us that elves are not an exclusively Western European fascination, with tracks such as 'Og'elend' and 'Return of the Nameless.'

Yet more lyrics and artists could be mentioned, but I'm sure you get the picture. Some readers may feel that a few of the bands listed have taken hardcore fan devotion to slavish and unnecessary extremes. Tom O'Dell demonstrated how aware he was of this when the publicity for *The Sons of Fëanor* wryly described him as "…walking the utterly untrodden path of Tolkien-based epic black metal." Another fan has joked that there is a metal band named after every place mentioned in the *Silmarillion;* it may well feel like that to readers. There have been several bands named after Sauron's tower, Barad Dur, for instance: the Italian group made clear their thraldom to *Lord of the Rings* when they released a demo titled 'Spectres over Isengard.'

What certainly can't be disputed is the devotion that Tolkien's books attract and the powerful inspiration that they provide. To many, elves and dwarves may sound like nothing more than empty fantasy, but the sheer volume of music being generated clearly indicates the continuing artistic vitality of Faery.

So far, much of the music that has been discussed has been created by heavy metal bands (of one description or another) who were drawn to the ideas and stories of Tolkien's work. We might marvel, too, at the fact that it is so substantially within the metal genre that these interests are expressed. It can be a violent, loud and muscular music that- on the face of it- is ill-suited to singing about faeries. This only reminds us how the faery has been overhauled on the last few decades. Out go (except for little girls at parties) pink flower faeries with wands and wings; in come elves, with cool hair and bows and arrows.

"Elvish singing is not a thing to miss..."

All the foregoing notwithstanding, some artists, however, have reacted to the Tolkien's epics by wishing to sound as if they *actually* come from Middle Earth. Jon Anderson, former vocalist of *Yes,* in 2006 collaborated with several other musicians and singers, collectively called 'The Fellowship,' to record *In Elven Lands,* a collection played on modern and antique instruments, such as the harp, lute, hurdy-gurdy and crumhorn, that was inspired by the writings of Tolkien. The haunting track 'Beware the Wolf' provides the album with its name: the song follows a hunter "through woven woods in elven lands."

Interviewed in August 2006 on the Howard Stern radio show in the USA, Anderson stated that he had acquired a spiritual adviser who "helped him see into the fourth dimension." He also revealed that, since a magic mushroom experience some time previously, he had considered himself to be part of the "elf culture."

On their album, 'The Fellowship' took a musicological approach to imagining how songs and tunes of the ancient cultures described by Tolkien might have sounded. The metre and style he employed for the verse in the books was copied for the tracks on the album (and, of course, the existence of these songs in the books provide both a template and a justification for all the bands we have considered to devise their own versions).  A variety of musical cultures inspired the different songs on *In Elven Lands*.  Thus, English folk tradition was drawn upon to represent Hobbit tunes; the elves' music was based on mediaeval sacred music and the ballads of the troubadours. The music of Numenor was like Elvish- but with added Greek and Macedonian influences. The results are truly striking.  The album cover, too, is notable: it uses an image from a medieval manuscript and Elvish lettering, but generally has a restrained tone, like an album of classical or early music.

The subject matter for the songs on *In Elven Lands* is drawn from numerous writings by Tolkien, not just *The Lord of the Rings* but *The Silmarillion*, *The Book of Lost Tales* and the *Unfinished Tales* as well.  The resulting tracks feature Quenya, Noldorin and Sindarin lyrics, alongside songs in modern English, Anglo-Saxon, and a kind of Neo-Elvish. Carvin Knowles, producer of *In Elven Lands,* has said of the recording process that "[Anderson] was a real sport about singing in Elvish... Hearing Sindarin with his Yorkshire accent is enough to make any fan smile." (NB: In fact, Anderson is from Accrington in Lancashire, a very important distinction if you're from either county...) The *Elven Lands* album also includes a cover of *Led Zeppelin*'s 'Battle of Evermore', transformed into a slow medieval ballad.

## "In the tongue of that land"

Projects similar to *In Elven Lands* are the Finnish *Middle Earth Band* and Aijin Hidelias' cover of 'Namarie: Galadriel's Lament,' which is helpfully available on *YouTube* with Quenya subtitles.  The same is the case for the *Forest Elves'* 'Elven Lullaby,' Anna Nym's *Mir Da'len Somniar* (Elvish Lullaby) and the *Tolkien Ensemble's* 'Galadriel.'[86]  The Spanish band, *Narsilion,* who were mentioned earlier, have released an

---

[86] The Ensemble have released four CDs: *An Evening in Rivendell* (1997), *A Night in Rivendell* (2000), *At Dawn in Rivendell* (2002), and (featuring Christopher Lee) *Leaving Rivendell* (2005).

interpretation of this song, *Namarie (El Llanto de Galadriel),* that is recorded partly in Spanish and partly in Quenya.

German metal band *Lyriel* included a track in Sindarin, 'Lind e-huil,' on their first studio album *Prisonworld*, which was released in 2005. The Swedes *Za Frûmi* are a project inspired by orcs and their language. The music derives from Norse folk tunes and features flutes, drums and ambient sound effects. The vocals are composed in the orcs' language, the *Black Speech*. The first CD in the '*Za Frumi Saga*' was released in 2000 and is titled *Za shum ushatar Uglakh* (The Great Warrior Uglakh); the project was concluded by *Shrak ishi za migul* ('Gathering in the Mist') in 2007.

These ventures into using and performing in Elvish speech aren't unique. Elves abound in the work of Norwegian black metal band *Burzum*, whose name means 'darkness' in the Black Speech of Mordor. *Twilight Force,* meanwhile, are a Swedish symphonic power metal band who even appear on stage in elf-ears and use Elvish in their songs, for instance in the sweeping and epic 'Heroes of Mighty Magic.' Amidst a swirling orchestration, a choir chants portentously:

> "Crying out for freedom
> Crying to the sky
> Ride on winds of ancient wisdom
> Pride in their hearts
>
> *Râd an dolen fili*
> *Im dû ned i raug*
> *Crist i aur a manadh*
> *Tog ti bâr.*"

The band have described themselves, and the *Heroes of Mighty Magic* album, in these terms: "*Twilight Force* is the intertwined destinies of six adventurers, on an endless quest to bring back glory, hope and sparkling magic to power metal, and to hopefully infuse the genre with new light, ideas and soundscapes never before experienced. It is a bombastic and merry journey, and one that we hope will bring much joy to humans, elves and dwarves in all mortal realms for a long time to come." *Twilight Force* have been supported on tour by fellow Swedes, *Sabaton.* Whilst they are perhaps best known for having a full-sized tank on stage for live performances, their song 'Shadows' is replete with references to Mordor, Sauron, halflings and hobbits.[87]

Lastly, dead languages as well as invented tongues have proved popular for various other metal bands who are also intrigued by fantasy themes. The Finnish folk metal *Ensiferum* (meaning 'sword bearing' in Latin) sing about witches, dragons and forests full of elves in 'Hero in a Dream.' *Nazgûl* are an Italian Tolkien-infused black metal band who, despite their name, write in Latin. Their 2002 album *De Expurgatione Elfmuth* included the epic track 'Elficidium' (Elf Slaughter) which describes a band of ogres raping and murdering elves before making off with their severed ears as trophies. 'Impetus Quartae Lunae Novae' describes an elvish battle.

## Earthly Elves

It might be argued that the elves of Middle Earth have rescued the faeries of British folklore from being surrendered entirely to children. For the last century and a half, the 'fairy' has increasingly come to signify a feminine, pretty and harmless being. Tolkien's elves, by way of contrast, are adult fare: they are martial, epic and adult. They engage in grown-up activities- fighting, scheming and sex- from which it follows that they can be regarded as a proper subject for adults- and perhaps especially males- to be interested in.

In several respects this revival of interest in mythology and supernatural beings may be welcome. Nevertheless, the elf of Middle Earth is *not* the faery of British folk tales. An enthusiasm for Legolas does not imply (at all) a liking too for Tom Tit Tot. Tolkien's elves are just that- they are an

---

[87] https://metalwani.com/2016/10/interview-twilight-forces-blackwald.html.

invention of Tolkien. They derive some physical and psychological traits from British and other elves, but they are not the same race of beings.

The key characteristics of the elves of Middle Earth are as follows. They are immortal and human sized. They reach maturity about the age of fifty and then will not die unless they are fatally injured (although they can recover from wounds that would kill humans) or unless they waste away through despair. They are tall and beautiful in face and body; they seem to shine with light. They have an ethereal grace, they walk lightly and can travel long distances without needing to sleep or even rest, enduring hardships and tiredness that the human body could not tolerate. They have better vision and hearing than humankind. They are skilled riders and have healing skills. The elves can make objects that are seemingly magical and which certainly possess certain special qualities. Certain elves can control nature and the elements. They are strictly monogamous.

The elves of Middle Earth have a number of noble traits and superhuman qualities, then, but they share very few of these with the faeries of British tradition. Both have very long life-spans that can only be terminated by fatal accident; some British faes are known for their acute hearing. However, whilst faery women are often renowned for their attractiveness, it is equally true that both sexes can be notably ugly (something Tolkien restricts to his dwarves). The British fae is, by and large, less than human in size and may be very small indeed. British faeries have healing skills and significant magical powers. The pixies are noted for their control over the weather, especially fogs and mists, but many of the faes are able to shape shift, or make themselves invisible- not known abilities of the elvish tribes of Middle Earth. Faeries are good riders, like the elves of Middle Earth, but they don't need to use their own legs or anyone else's: they can simply travel through the air using enchanted items. British faeries are particularly known for their promiscuous natures and for their changeable and frequently mischievous (but sometimes vindictive or vengeful) temperaments.

In summary, Tolkien borrowed a handful of the aspects of his elves from British folklore, but much he made up- or elaborated. The widespread popularity of *Lord of the Rings,* therefore, whether in music or any other sphere of the arts, is in a real sense quite detached from the consideration of the role of 'faeries' that forms the theme of this book.[88]

---

[88] See, for example, my *Faery Lifecycle* and *The Darker Side of Faery* (2021), *British Fairies* (2017) and *Faery* (2020).

# Fade Out: "Beyond the Fields We Know"

This examination of the influence of the faery mythology on (largely) British and English-speaking music reveals a strange fact. Most of the fae sources upon which writers and musicians have drawn were not actually part of British folk tradition. The Irish *sidhe,* classical *nymphs, naiads* and *dryads*, and literary or artistic representations of faeries have made a far greater impression than the material to be found in folklore collections. Of course, this is hardly to be wondered at: most of those originally oral stories are relatively hard of access (or, at least, were). Famous paintings and the works of Machen, Tolkien and Dunsany could be accessed through any decent book shop or library. The result is (although we should hardly expect otherwise) that the songs created are, by and large, further contributions to the imaginative literature rather than being any sort of faerylore document.

This is not to disparage them: renewed power, reach and relevance are given to the stories by each fresh recension and, more significantly, each new faery song or opera only serves to strengthen and sustain the hold that faerylore, myth and legend have upon our collective imaginations. Periodically, in every generation, people declare that Faery has passed away- that it is a belief of older people like their grandparents. Hopefully, this book shows how mistaken that is.

Another difference between some of the early twentieth century composers and later musicians is the (apparent) lack of personal faery experiences. One particularly surprising exception to this, however, involves John Rutledge, a rapper from the Newport hip-hop group *Goldie Lookin' Chain.* In June 2016 it was widely reported that he encountered- and photographed- some fairies during a walk in the countryside near Newbridge, north of Caerffili. On the face of it, the post-industrial valleys of South Wales are an inauspicious area to meet the *tylwyth teg,* but, on reviewing the pictures he'd taken after he had returned home, Rutledge saw what looked like seven tiny winged creatures flying among the flowers and grass. They were translucent figures, about four centimetres in height and with arms and legs as well as wings. The unlikelihood of a rapper seeing a faery (and admitting it) may tend to persuade us of his veracity.

The faeries are still out there, then, and that is why we are still driven to sing about them. They conjure up images of simpler times, when problems were, perhaps, more easily solved by the application of courage and daring.

Of course, the fascination with supernatural beings runs wholly counter to the superficial rationality and materialism of the age, an indication of the fact that many people are unhappy with the roles and rules with which they must live. They seek vehicles to express aspirations that aren't easily accommodated within modern society and to verbalise doubts about the direction of the global economy. Faeries and elves offer a means of framing those anxieties. Unlikely, then, as it may seem, they are a form of protest song.

## Further Reading

You can listen to all *Tyrannosaurus Rex*'s albums on *YouTube*, of course; check out too the work of almost all the other artists I have discussed.

For more information on Marc Bolan, see these biographies:

Paul Roland, *Cosmic Dancer,* 2012;
Mark Paytress, *Marc Bolan- The Rise and Fall of a Twentieth Century Superstar,* 2003; and,
John Bramley, *Marc Bolan- Beautiful Dreamer,* 2017.

For John Peel, see his autobiography *Margrave of the Marches* (2006) and
Michael Heatley, *John Peel,* 2004.

Valuable and highly enjoyable general texts are Simon Reynolds, *Shock and Awe* and Rob Young's *Electric Eden.*

See the WordPress site https://nakedonastrangeplanet.com/ for a very comprehensive Marc Bolan/ T. Rex blog.

Mike Barne's *New Day Yesterday* is an excellent study of progressive rock in its social and musical context.

## Coda One- Freddie Mercury's Inspiration

As described in my chapter on seventies rock, the *Queen* vocalist Freddie Mercury was inspired to write a song on the subject of the picture, *The Fairy Feller's Master Stroke*, both by repeatedly visiting Richard Dadd's painting in the Tate Gallery and by closely reading the explanatory verse the painter composed to accompany it. To better understand the origin of the track, that poem is presented in full and analysed here. It is titled an *Elimination* by Dadd, in other words- an elucidation of the meaning of his picture, his limning.

Richard Dadd (1817-1886) had been a promising painter before a trip made to the Middle East and Egypt in 1842. During this journey, he began to show signs of acute mental distress and, upon his return to England in 1843, he murdered his father and was committed for life to the Bethlem hospital. Whilst there, he was not regarded as a serious threat to staff or other inmates and was allowed to continue with his painting as part of his therapy. During this time, Dadd produced several remarkable fairy images, each of which took several years to complete. The *Fairy Feller's Master Stroke* is one of these. The artist wrote the poem explaining its meaning for

George Henry Haydon, who was head steward of the hospital and had commissioned the painting.

The poem itself meanders in a somewhat aimless and, at times, confusing manner from subject to subject- until it commences its figure-by-figure analysis of the painting (at which point the reader is advised to have a copy of the picture to hand in order to follow Dadd has he works methodically around the canvas, from bottom to top- or, in the picture's plane, front to back). His diction can be unique and difficult from time to time, too.

*Elimination of a picture and its subject- called the Feller's Master Stroke* (Broadmoor, January 1865)[89]

"Half twelve, that's six, 'tis more
Perhaps, exact that's gone before
Behoves not here to say,
How many years away
Have welled up and flowed on
Slow passing till they're gone.[90]
But some such time has fled
Since regular business led
To where a canvas glowed
With fays, a leafy node
Encircling wild about.
Their differences they let out
About an Indian boy,[91]
Whom for a toy,
To while the time
Or teach to mime
Or verse in fairy tricks,
A mighty King his eyes did fix

---

[89] The picture was completed in 1864; Dadd was then transferred to the newly opened Broadmoor hospital- hence the ascription.

[90] Perhaps Dadd's guess at how long he'd been confined.

[91] This is a clear reference to the 'changeling child' over which Titania and Oberon dispute in Shakespeare's *Midsummer Night's Dream*, which is set outside Athens.

Upon with covetous regard;
When met upon the sward,
Near Athen's learned seat [92]
His Queen had set her feet
Thrice happy green.  Business
Led, an official person to this sight [93]
Who with the picture pleased,
As 't'were a jewel bright,
His mind of burden eased,
To have the like
Of which did strike,
At fancy's shrine well meant.
If 'twas not so, then I may say
'Twas this perhaps, that west away
Some friend he had, who wrote in verse
About the fairies, sense as terse
As poets jam into a measured line
And gives such extra value I opine
To Heliconian jet so of his rhymes [94]
Possessed, he wished to see
A little sketch, slight as may be
To illustrate the same-
Some stanzas shewed as game
Or point from which to throw.
Sees nothing clearly, as his has
Blackly impositive and soon
Makes it as clear as sunny noon
That he has not.

Waiting this heavenly gift [95]
I thought on nought- a shift
As good perhaps as thinking hard.
Fancy was not to be evoked
From her ethereal realms

---

[92] *A Midsummer Night's Dream* is set, of course, in a wood near Athens.
[93] A description of the commission by George Henry Haydon follows.
[94] Mount Helicon is home to the Muses.
[95] Dadd describes how he was inspired to paint.

Or if so, then her purpose cloaked
And nuzzling the cloth, on which
The cloudy shades not rich,
Indefinite, almost unseen,
Lay vacant entities of chance,
Lent forms unto my careless glance
Without intent; pure fancy 'tis I mean.
Design and composition thus-
Now minus and just here perhaps- plus-
Grew in this way- and so- or thus,
That fairly wrought they stand in view.
A fairy band, much as I say, just so 'tis true.
Part from the shades designed
Part a vain fancy, all inclined
A common end to gain
Of nothing something still
To stand before, the sight to fill
Something we have, having, we
Yet have not
Be it so or nay, why care a jot?
But there they are- and now
They stand a theme- a field to plough
And silent reap what any choose
Judiciously or not to lose.[96]
All, the significance may give
They surely think in this doth live.
As Nature's Pages open spread
By erudite or fools are read,
To this one seems the world a den
While that a paradise in it doth ken
In the same place, 'tis lore
Pre-acquisite,[97] the wise man's store
Gives off a value rich and full
To that sprung from a sense so dull
It does not half appreciate
Upon that which it doth dilate.

---

[96] Every viewer can interpret the picture as s/he wishes.
[97] Meaning, presumably, already acquired.

Dilatory, dull, absorbing, rapt
In the sort of a kind of a something mapped
While struggling reason roams away
Nor will in such dull fetters stay
But leaves the author out of himself
To make his fame or gain his pelf
If so he may- or can-
But to the common mind
The meaning thus, let's find.

For idle pastime hither led
Fays, gnomes, and elves and suchlike fled
To fix some dubious point to fairies only
Known to exist, or to the lonely
Thoughtful man recluse
Of power a potent spell to loose
Which binds the better slave to worse
Swindles soul, body, goods and purse
T'unlock the secret cells of dark abyss
The power which never doth its victim miss
But may egorge when truth appears [98]
When fail or guns or swords or spears.

For some such end we may suppose
They've met since day hath made its close
Night's noon time haply extra bright
By fairie power made all so light
Doubtful if night or day might reign
To certain be in mind revolve again
And say that common nature is not true.
Precisely to what fairie opes to view
Comme ça for the effect, if you should doubt.
If you've not been there, perhaps you mought [must]
Make a fresh bend; we'll now advance
These folk displayed as in a trance
Have not the dexter object here
But the same might be sinister

---

[98] This is, I think, Dadd's own word- exgorge, i.e. disgorge.

For saintly doubtless it is rare
To call a goblin elf, the lair
He loves, or any thing or sprite
That in the name of fairy doth delight-
Or e'en the land itself-
Laden with un-impossible wealth;
To the mutton says Monsieur Crapaud [99]

This meet unto the Patriarch owed [100]
Say its conclave- and here to shew
His triple crown of subtle might
Weird in its form & shining bright
An arch magician whose large little club
Of some hard heavy wood is but a stubb
And might be loaded in its larger butt
Force to add when to use 'tis put
But even without no fairy skull
Resist it might however thick or dull
A little bit of wood just a mere twig
For which a plodding mortal less than a fig
Cares- but to an elf it has
A power as fatal as the Upas.[101]
If on a sudden it descends
On fairy sconce, its revel ends
And then you know poor little fart
Unto another private realm he will depart.
"Don't want to hurt poor little fa-er-ee"
Appeals the rogue unto the powers that be
The arch-fiend sees no dodge illicit
'Bout younker caught- is not explicit
Or he might say "Don't let me catch you here again
Or perhaps you'll meet with far too much sharp pain
And stunning effects the same to follow-
Which will not leave you time to holloa!"

---

[99] A derogatory term for a French person- 'Mr Toad' as in 'Froggies.' "To the mutton"- let's get down to business.
[100] The wizard seated at the centre of picture.
[101] A poisonous Asiatic tree.

Beneath his wide spread crown
He casts a glance adown
Dim vistas of the pregnant coming bustle
To note if there is aught to stay or hustle
The incident peculiar here
Inciding edge incising clear
Or so to do.
His right hand raised, seems to declare
"Except I tell you when, strike if you dare –
For all the powers of skill or chance
Fairies can use before my glance-
are bare"
'Tis so- no doubt, but even Almighty Power
Suffers defeat each day and every hour
As unforeseen some little trifling thing
Cheats of a stave another song we sing
His glance means likely too
If t'other is not much ado
He with one blow, another turn will serve
If from the aim's intent it doth not swerve
Left to its time and how to do
To split, for Mab perchance a chariot new.[102]
'Tis all the skill there is for such a deed
Happen, happening in faerie for fairy's need.

See- 'tis fay woodman holds aloft the axe
Whose double edge virtue now they tax
To do it single & make single double
Teatly and neatly- equal without trouble
'Tis not yet done- yet there he stands
Try if he'll do it- for your own commands
He knows the axe to use on fairy trees
And fairy common sense embodies if you please
If that your fancy you can strain so far.
As to suppose the same and yet not mar
Your mental method and decorum

---

[102] The whole point of the picture is that an acorn is being split to make a new carriage for Queen Mab.

138

Where all things shew them *quasi coram* [103]
He's clothed in leather note from top to toe.
All of one colour you may mark also.
The colour of his money you might say.
Good or bad adding lack-a-day.
How can I tell?
Splitting is either good or bad
For not so the same terms are had.
And that's his money so to speak
Merely though 'tis about a freak.
As to the colour this we'll add
'Tis warm enough for fairy mad
But fairy leather comes from victims small.
Though if they're cattle fed in field or stall,
I know not – or bat's wings dyed to suit the taste
But to the next one let us haste.[104]

The ostler from the fairy inn [105]
Knowing his air, the curate of the trim
Hands to his knees and body bent
On the nuts so tiny is all intent
With well spurred heel can ride a-main
Stirrup or saddle seeks not to maintain
His seat the which so well he knows
Secure the menage that around him grows
That is a look of mastery as 't-were to say
There is no dodge to me doth lay
Concealed where asses dogs or varmint be,
I am a doctor veterinaree
They call me night or morn as 't eve
Tom- price-
I know full well of beasts and in a trice
Your servant Sir your ass I'll groom
And shew you to the fairy inn's best room.

---

[103] "as before"
[104] Readers may recall that the fairies in *Midsummer Night's Dream* hunt bats for the leather of their wings (Act 2, scene 2).
[105] The ostler is owner of a hostelry- a pub or tavern.

What are you at there? Steady ho!!!
Do you think his gaze will help the blow?

Next a dwarf monk with shaven crown
On the bank's brink hath cast adown
His wide sleeved arms and rests his chin
Partly his face his hands conceal-
I put him in- For why?
Because I may reply
Monk's beatific mount they say on high.
But as historians do over
About their manners some demur
Checks the free access unto Heaven
And then, of that to speak with leaven
Of circumspection, unto a nether
Region they adhere.
Not holding on to it very tight, I fear.
And where there is but little wine or beer.
Far wandering habits also 'tis well known
Led the same blades about from town to town
And this with inns- and sutlers too- [106]
Familiarly acquainted grew.
Says he's a rogue & to the next-

'Tis varhma's ploughman claims the text.[107]
He has a twinkle in his eye
Bespeaks good humour you'll descry
Of cows and sheep & crops can talk
Quite wonderful & see him walk
With lounging stride across the fields
Just turned afresh to raise the crop that yields.
Ample return for all his labour
That wants no sound of pipe and tabour.
His doubtful speech he hath addressed
To Waggoner Will beside him, lest
The sage remark quite lost should be.

---

[106] Sutlers supply provisions to an army.
[107] A mock dialect version of 'farmer.'

But how indifferent Will is- see!
Come hither! Woah is more to him
Than such a speculative whim

Above Clod-hopper sits and like the sod-
He's brown in colour, also he's well shod.
A satyr's head has, buckles in his shoes;
Nurses one foot upon his knee amuse with him
Yourself he's modern fay.
So gives his garb and decent sylvan he.
Is not stark naked and so proud might be
A foot and not a hoof to own.
But can he put a hat upon his crown?
His horns forbid- say that it slid
From off his pate and fell
Where! he nor I can tell!
There let it lie-

The Politician next, with senatorial pipe,
For argument or his opinion ripe.
A first chop Englishman at that sort of chaff.
To hear him talk, Lord!
How 't-would make you laugh.
For fairy politics differ so very wide
From human governments complete divide.
He's pondering matters now as if his vote
Ought to be given ere 'tis smote.
The nut – I mean –

Next him observe one clad in green-
An unknown character, some fairy dandy,
Making a break as sweet as candy
To faery nymph like him so quaint.
They are poor ones clearly and attaint.
The present case, because 'tis queer,
And like themselves- yet no small beer-
They deem of their own station.

Behind them elves quite wide awake

Notes of the doings here to take
And to their fellows bye and bye
Tell all without a word of a lie.

Below a pedagogue appears.
A Critic up to sneers and jeers.
And by his faun-like ears he's wild
Untamed himself, each fairy child
He tames with many a look severe
But if his glance is there or here
'Tis hard to say. He squints to note
You may. But he'll not meddle
With a work so sharp.
Waits in suspense and doth not carp.
His business is to teach to do.
Do it himself? Oh no! 'tis you.

Next come two wenches rather smart.
From lady's chamber where each art
Of fairy luxury they the care,
At madam's need, can well prepare.
This holds a mirror in her hand so tiny-
A magic surface polished bright & shiny-
While that a broom to sweep away
The fairy rubbish lack-a-day
Holds in her left hand; on her right
A favourite hawk moth doth alight.
They've got good legs and feet so small-
Bavaria Flanders Germany and all
Can shew no more fantastic limb.
Critics are severe 'tis therefore that I beg.
You'll not inform that fay, that under the leg
Of one of those maids, behind her back,
A satyr peeps; at what, it doth not lack,
An explanation.
At such a book,
His right to look,
I care not to dispute.
Such secrets surely some must know.

All are not saints on earth below-
Or if they are- they know the same,
Or are shut out from nature's game;
Banished from nature's book of life,
Because some angel in the strife
Had got the worser fate.
And they close their eyes, that gate
By which reminders enter
And in a paradise of fools contented live.
Fays also are not saints, so I must believe
That this and similar frolics they achieve.
The truth is not for all you'll say
But that eternal seal it bear,
One might say nay.
Who are the victims of that cruel fate
False secrecy, that sometimes 'tis too late
To find- lost to their race for ever they
In other spheres can understand the light of day.[108]

Next Lubin bending o'er his flame-
Chloe or Phyllis- hard to tame,[109]
With wooden sabots round about she'll clatter.
Churn fairy butter or some such matter.
As to the dairy doth belong
Whiling and charming time with song.[110]
They're rustic lovers- rustic in manner.
And Lubin happen is a fairy tanner,
Tanned woodman's leather coat and cap,
His leggins, all their boots mayhap.
Except his sweethearts they are of wood,
He'd do them too to oblige her if he could.
They are curious in this business you see plainly.

---

[108] The preceding paragraph makes reference to the theory that faeries are fallen angels, who became trapped between heaven and hell when the doors of each were sealed.
[109] Conventional names for Arcadian- i.e. country- girls.
[110] The association of faeries with dairies and their products is traditional.

See also next below, two dwarfs- ungainly?
No for the sake of rhyme it fits so well-
We'll write it down- and after tell
That 'tis deformity approaches near
The truth about this couple here.
A fairy conjuror he who knows a trick
Or two at cards and in the nick
Of time, can well deceive-
Thus, of your reason you take leave.
Then 'tis that he will do the clever dodge.
Which puzzles many a clownish varhma Hodge.
You think perhaps you don't do so.
The prayer book so affirms I know-
Just now he offers out to let-
'Twill or 'twill not be surely split.
Some odds perhaps will give
What fairy coin is- true as I live
I can't inform- nor if they betted
And if they did, the profits netted.

The spider near his web hath left,
Drops down upon them from some cleft
Where he spread his wide snare for game
One that detains yet doth not maim
Perhaps he's an offer when they have done.
To supply with gossamer wells all, every one.
A master weaver he in whose employ
The lesser spinners may enjoy
Profits and learn to make account
Of those who wish aloft to mount.
And sail away upon the wind
From Europe p'raps to furthest Ind.
They've only wind to ask for- 'tis the weather
That in this case saves the expense of leather
And pilgrimages- let's make one
To the opposite side- that is, objection
If you've none- two braves we see,
In gallantry, who by their wits can live-
Can sing or play- fight, run away,

Or entertainment give.
Your fairy man upon the town.
That can clean out a swell or clown.
And if there's need can let you down
A peg or two- so high they fly.
Hawking while talking all my eye.

Next to the Patriarch's
Crown attend. And mark the motes
That there descend.
Dancing and singing there they go
With their *fal lal the rah* and *huy gee wohe*.
The dress is Spanish 'tis in use,
At present time If I abuse,
Not memory of the source
From which I borrowed them of course
Call cottagers, no bloods are, these;
As on a tight rope they to please.
I represented – when in the play
One is dressed like to Duvernay.

Balancing these on the other side
Queen Mab in car of state doth ride.
Some atomies the poet says did draw[111]
A gnat gives to them coachman's law.
I never saw the famed Queen Mab, or might,
Had it been so contributed delight.
The atomies are, no doubt, a dubious theme-
Like tiny female centaurs here do seem.
Half beast and half a woman yoked are,
With wings to soar away in regions far.
Under the coachman standing nigh
Two little pages you may spy.
Cupid and Psyche they enact,
Fairies no doubt possess the tact
To imitate like mortal players

---

[111] A reference to Mercutio's description of Mab in *Romeo & Juliet,* Act 1, scene 4.

I know not if at theatres or fairs.
It needs must be so-
Fairies 'tis said shun all display
And most affect the pale moon's ray[112]
Sol's potent ray soon drives them off
He'd instant find whereat to spurn and scoff-
Just so it was with folk in olden time,
Whose practices were held to be a crime.
They fled the powers that held despotic sway-
Poor little fairies! why not also they?
Fancy this pair aught else 'twill do,
But male and female they are plain to view.

Next to the Queen you here behind may count,
Some strapping fairy footmen mount
And *garde chemin* no doubt they well do serve.[113]
Tiny in size but lusty in the nerve,
As every footman should be.

Above, in attitude of fondest love,
King Oberon & his Queen approve
The sport- else why should they repair
To this sequestered spot the same to share
Merely- perhaps- to note the way things went.
And how many chops were useless made anent.
Pulling of straws out from a stack of wheat.
Is for a pastime not more meet.

And such the Old Lady in the Scarlet Cloak,
Might non-be fancying true- no joke.
Is it true for me or even you-
True if you care not- this is true.
Her nose and chin will never crack
The monster nuts & many a whack
From club or shining axe will want

---

[112] The very common belief that fairies emerge only after dark- and
preferably on moonlit nights.
[113] Servants to protect the queen during her journey.

Ere the chance fatal lights upon't

Above the harridan some whose names
Serve schoolboys turn when at their games
They of the future calling prophecy
With boisterous laugh and ecstasy
Of childish mirth, nor want they
Perhaps a forced imposed belief.
In soldier and sailor, tinker or tailor
Ploughboy, apothecary, thief.
Counting their buttons down the vest.
A name to each- the last doth rest
The faded rade- soon from the thoughts 'tis laid
Aside and fairy prophecy forgot.
Here let me say my let of this same lot:
The ragged soldier sure is mad:
Made so by wounds, debauch and glad
But hard-earned victory
Being fay, I've not the history.
I made it so but not from spite,
Else he'd find reason to requite
But ragamuffins to enlist.
He's a brave spirit to assist.
Knows when he does he'll be Commander,
The chief one, or a Salamander.
A real fire eater like the Sun
By his own bravery surely won.
The sailor keeps a pleasure yacht
Has nought to do but live on what
The smiling elements that never frown
Freely disclose as up and down
For pleasure merely roam about
The fleets of vessels of which he'll take
Entire command for the nation's sake,
Nor cares he where to move or swim.
'Till death commands to dowse the glim.
Some other oceans then he'll try,
Rolling eternal in the sky.

The tinker next with barrow trig
Knows every wandering gypsy rig
Where does he lodge? 'tis hard to say
Whether a house or stack of hay
Serves the poor outcast for his rest.
He's butt howe'er for many a jest,
Lives in a world of nether pose
Mysterious obscure, your senses lose
Or cast aside as nothing worth
Nor length it has nor breadth or girth
Just now he marks the filbert big
Stript of its natural russet wig
How would he here his skill to prove?
He'd grind it p'raps? Not so by Jove
Clumsily skilful though he be
He knows too much for that, d'ye see?
Around the fairy villages he'll stray
Knives, scissors to grind might bawl each day.
Knows well the tailor reg'lar grinds his shears.

Ah! That's a tailor brave that knows no fears.
Nine fairy tailors would not make a man
Tho' they might queer him; you know well they can.
But this one seems disposed to queer,
The plough-boy that is standing to him near
Shews him a coat neat made and very strong
'T would last the lad his fairy life time long.[114]
But while he doubts the same to buy,
The thief his craft on him doth try.
Loosens his handkerchief so gay.
Too artful he to snatch away.

The doctor, in his thoughts reserved,
The trick below hath not observed
But with his sounding pestle beats,
The drugs that he to fairy metes.

---

[114] Faeries are very long-lived, though probably not immortal- see my *Faery Lifecycle,* 2021.

His mortar would not hold the nut.
But holds enough for fairy gut.
A nostrum or a panacea
At any price we'll say not dear.

Next to the soldier, on his right,
A dragonfly exerts his skill and might
Sounds the long notes 'long the long tube that wind
And in the fairy hollows echoes find.

To assist this gaudy long legged trumpeter
A tatteredemalion and a junketer,[115]
Holiday folk that tends upon,
Like a postilion if you con
Each blows his brazen tube no doubt in tune
With dragonfly that rests his leg abune
The jutting stone on which they sit
Expecting company that soon will flit
Slanting along the lunar ray
Like boys and girls come out to play.

A-low behind these last-named two
An elfin takes a peeping view-
Not at the nut but the spectator
Happen to mark if arbitrator
He in this remarkable fudge
Or humbug gives the fatal nudge.
Peeper is wildest of the crew
Cares nought for them or I or you.
You from his cap with me perchance agree
Of the Chinese Small Foot Societee,
He's a small member.
But if Confucius sent him
Now I can't remember.

Turn to the Patriarch and behold
Long pendents from his crown are rolled,

---

[115] Mercury directly quoted from this line.

In winding figures circle round
The grass and such upon the mound,
They represent vagary wild
And mental aberration styled.
Now unto nature clinging close
Now wildly out away they toss,
Like a cyclone uncontrolled
Sweeping around with chance-born fold
Unto the picture brings a grace
Which else was wanting to its face
But tied at length unto a stem
Shews or should do *finitam rem.*[116]

The size the nuts do here display
Forgive nor make me forfeit pay
Having the benefit of doubt
Of what the fairies grow without
The reach of human ken or will
And needs not now that I instil
Into your mind.
What here I've said from fancy's wing
A sense supporting of my need
You may deny- say- no such thing
'Tis all wrong every bit indeed.
Well! to your judgment I must bow-
Freely its exercise allow;
You, perhaps, to such are more inured-
Your notions may be more endured;
But, whether it be or be not so,
You can afford to let this go
For nought as nothing it explains
And nothing, from nothing, nothing gains."

---

[116] To conclude matters.

# Coda Two- Glossarium Metallicum

For readers less familiar with the either the style, or with the various sub-genres of heavy metal, I thought it might be helpful to include a short glossary of terms- those that are most relevant to faery and fantasy related themes.

There are many other types of heavy metal, such as 'death metal' and 'thrash,' which we need not describe here. Notable, though, is the common singing style known as the 'death growl,' a technique devised over time by the vocalists of a number of death metal bands. It's significant here as it can be heard on several Middle Earth or fantasy tracks, very effectively representing the voices of Sauron, orcs or other 'evil' characters.

*Black metal* is an extreme subgenre of heavy metal. Common features of the style are very fast tempos, shrieked vocals, heavy guitar distortion and unconventional song structures. The musicians may assume pseudonyms and on-stage identities with costumes and face paint. It has been especially associated with the Scandinavian countries and with pagan or Satanist themes. The genre may be further analysed into ambient, industrial, grindcore, Viking, symphonic, psychedelic and dungeon synth.

*Folk metal* is a genre of heavy metal fusing that style of rock with traditional folk European music. The use of folk instruments and, less commonly, traditional singing styles is typical. Medieval, Celtic and Oriental subgenres have emerged within the style.

*Power metal* is a subgenre of heavy metal that combines the characteristics of traditional heavy metal with those of speed metal, often within a symphonic context. Generally, power metal has a faster, lighter, and more uplifting sound, in contrast with the heaviness and dissonance commonly found in extreme metal. Power metal bands usually have anthem-like songs with strong choruses, thus creating a theatrical, dramatic and emotionally affecting sound. Power metal is known for its triumphant, mythological and heroic themes; bands often devise their own fantastical worlds and release concept albums dealing with warriors and dragons.

*Symphonic metal* is a style found within several sub-genres of heavy metal. The term's applied to any metal band that makes use of symphonic or orchestral elements (and even instruments). The style combines the recognisable heavy drums and guitars of metal with different elements from classical music, such as orchestral scores and choirs, albeit most commonly using synthesisers to reproduce these. Many such bands use classically trained (often female) vocalists, giving rise, too, to labels such as opera metal or operatic metal.

Made in the USA
Monee, IL
26 May 2023